T0314937

HANDBOOK OF
LGBT TOURISM
AND HOSPITALITY

A GUIDE FOR BUSINESS PRACTICE

ABOUT THE AUTHORS

Jeff Guaracino and Ed Salvato are leaders in the LGBT travel industry. They are friends, business partners, global speakers, and thought leaders in the travel, hospitality, and publishing industries. To research this book, Guaracino and Salvato traveled to six continents, interviewed nearly a hundred industry experts and hundreds of LGBT travelers, and observed emerging trends.

JEFF GUARACINO is an expert in destination tourism marketing and large-scale events. His interest in the field of LGBT travel started in 2002, when he attended Community Marketing's International LGBT Tourism and Hospitality Conference in Miami, Florida.

Serving as the vice president of communications for the Greater Philadelphia Tourism Marketing Corporation (GPMTC) from 2001 until 2012, he led the team that created Philadelphia's groundbreaking campaign, Philadelphia Get Your History Straight and Your Nightlife Gay®. That award-winning campaign set a new record for effectiveness and return on investment, and it made history with many LGBT marketing firsts, among them the debut of the world's first television commercial for a destination for the LGBT traveler. Guaracino's work in the tourism and hospitality industry in all LGBT segments and beyond has been noted by more than fifty prestigious travel industry awards.

Guaracino went on to become the executive director of the Atlantic City Alliance, a private, nonprofit destination marketing organization for Atlantic City, New Jersey, from 2012 to 2016. The herculean challenge was to reposition Atlantic City beyond its sole reliance on gaming to a year-round resort destination and to thereby reverse the destination's dramatic tourism decline. LGBT tourism became one segment that helped Atlantic City start its comeback.

In 2016 Philadelphia's Mayor Jim Kenney named Guaracino president and CEO of Welcome America, Inc., in Philadelphia. Guaracino's first book, *Gay and Lesbian Tourism: The Essential Guide for Marketing,* is often considered the must-have, go-to resource on LGBT tourism marketing. He writes a syndicated travel column and speaks around the world. Guaracino can be reached at LGBTexpert.com

ED SALVATO is a journalist, author, public speaker, and content expert. Having graduated from Harvard with a degree in applied mathematics and economics and from Northeastern University with an MBA in market research, Salvato began his career as a market researcher and then moved on to travel journalism, believing that both careers require the same tactics for success: gathering and analyzing data and writing insightful analyses. Since 2012 he has served as chief content officer of *ManAboutWorld*, the world's number-one digital gay travel magazine for tablets and smartphones. He was previously editor in chief (from 1998 to 2004) of the groundbreaking subscription-based printed newsletter *Out&About,* which was the first gay travel editorial product with a consumer (rather than an advertiser) focus. In 2004 he was appointed corporate director of travel media for PlanetOut Inc., overseeing travel content at Gay.com, PlanetOut.com, OutTraveler.com, Advocate.com, *Advocate* magazine, and Alyson Publications (now Alyson Books). During that time he was also editor in chief of *Out Traveler* and a contributing editor for *Out* magazine. He assembles and moderates the annual consumer LGBT panel at the *New York Times* Travel Show and the Adventure and Travel Shows in a number of their markets, including Washington, D.C., and Philadelphia.

HARRINGTON PARK PRESS

NEW YORK, NY • USA   YORK, NORTH YORKSHIRE • UK

JEFF GUARACINO
ED SALVATO

HANDBOOK OF LGBT TOURISM AND HOSPITALITY

A GUIDE FOR BUSINESS PRACTICE

Harrington Park Press
Box 331
9 East Eighth Street
New York, NY 10003

Library of Congress Cataloging-in-Publication Data

Names: Guaracino, Jeff, author. | Salvato, Ed, 1962– author.
Title: Handbook of LGBT tourism & hospitality : a guide for business practice / Jeff Guaracino, Ed Salvato.
Other titles: Handbook of LGBT tourism and hospitality | Handbook of lesbian, gay, bisexual, and transgender tourism and hospitality
Description: New York, NY : Harrington Park Press, [2017]
Identifiers: LCCN 2016039349 (print) | LCCN 2016058875 (ebook) | ISBN 9781939594181 (hardcover : alk. paper) | ISBN 9781939594174 (softcover : alk. paper) | ISBN 9781939594198 (ebook)
Subjects: LCSH: Gays—Travel. | Tourism—Management.
Classification: LCC HQ75.25 .G833 2017 (print) | LCC HQ75.25 (ebook) | DDC 306.76/6—dc23
LC record available at https://lccn.loc.gov/2016039349

Manufactured in the United States of America

10 9 8 7 6 5 4 3 2 1

This book is dedicated to our family, friends, mentors, and the LGBT pioneers in travel and civil rights.

LGBT TRAVEL EXPERTS AND ADVISERS

The authors wish to thank the panel of experts and advisers who provided their suggestions for the best practices in the world of LGBT travel. We'd like especially to acknowledge:

Martine Ainsworth-Wells, Ainsworth & Wells (formerly Visit London/London & Partners)

Tom Alderink, Belmond

Jon Allen, Island House Resort Key West

Tracy Baim, *Windy City Times*

Alan Beck, FunMaps

Michael Bertetto, SLS Las Vegas (formerly with Wynn Las Vegas and Encore and R&R Partners)

Rich Campbell, Atlantis Events

Felipe Cardenas, Colombian LGBT Chamber of Commerce

Clovis Casemiro, 4 Go Travel network

Tanya Churchmuch, Much PR (formerly with Tourism Montreal)

Brad Cicero, Porter Airlines

Joe D'Alessandro, San Francisco Convention and Visitors Bureau

Alexis Dee, Southern Comfort

Pablo DeLuca, GNetworks360

Fred Dixon, NYC & Company

Stuart Elliott, MediaVillage (formerly with the *New York Times*)

Alfredo Ferreyra, BUEGay Argentina

Apoorva Gandhi, Marriot International, Inc.

Gina Gatta, Damron LGBT Travel Guides

David Gonzalez, MGM Resorts International

Richard Gray, Greater Fort Lauderdale Convention and Visitors Bureau

Richard Green, BestBus

Randy Griffin, Marshall Hotels (formerly with Marriott International)

Malcolm Griffiths, Development Counsellors International

Nicki Grossman, Greater Fort Lauderdale Convention and Visitors Bureau

Charlie Gu, China Luxury Advisors

Christina Guggenberger, formerly Stockholm Visitors Board, City of Stockholm

Greg Hamman, Underseas Expeditions

Keith Hart, World OutGames Miami 2017

Bryan Herb, Zoom Vacations

Masaki Higashida, Beyond Tokyo

Shiho Ikeuchi, Hotel Granvia Tokyo

Rika Jean-François, ITB Berlin

David Jefferys, Altus Agency

Merryn Johns, *Curve*

Ian Johnson, Out Now Global and Out Now Business Class

Gregg Kaminsky, R Family Vacations

Betti Keese, GoBeyond—Women's Travel and LezTrek

Donna Keren, NYC & Company

Brian King, Marriott International

Robert Klara, *AdWeek*

Shintaro Koizumi, Out Asia Travel

Billy Kolber, *ManAboutWorld* Magazine

Ron Kuijpers, Gay Tours Mexico

Meryl Levitz, Visit Philadelphia (formerly known as Greater Philadelphia Tourism Marketing Corporation, GPTMC)

Russell Lord, Kenes Tours

Christy Mallory, Williams Institute

Auston Matta, Two Bad Tourists

Michael McDowell, Los Angeles Tourism and Convention Board

Ryan Miccio, United Airlines

Miles Mitchinson, Detours Travel

Zachary Moses, HE Travel

Jonathan Mountford, Made Travel

Jon Munoz, Hilton Worldwide

Rick Murray, Crown & Anchor

George Neary, Miami Convention and Visitors Board

Dean Nelson, Whistler Pride and Ski Festival

Gustavo Noguera, GNetworks360

Clint Ostler, Alaska Airlines

David Paisley, Community Marketing & Insights

Yolanda Perdomo, United Nations World Tourism Organization

Joseph Poteet, Kimpton Hotels & Restaurants

Catherine Reilly, Brendan Vacations

Mya Reyes, Las Vegas Gay Visitors Bureau

Mark C. Romig, New Orleans Tourism Marketing Corporation

Steve Roth, Alturi (formerly with OutThink Partners and Atlantis Events)

Tom Roth, Community Marketing & Insights

Charlie Rounds, Wiser Wolf (formerly with OutThink Partners and RSVP Vacations)

David Ryan, Rhino Africa Safaris

Darrell Schuurman, Travel Gay Canada

Mark Segal, *Philadelphia Gay News*

Robert Sharp, Out Adventures

Michael F. Sheridan, Temple University, School of Sport, Tourism and Hospitality Management

Eric Silverberg, SCRUFF

Rajat Singla, Pink Vibgyor, India

Matt Skallerud, Pink Banana Media

Bernadette Smith, The Equality Institute

Craig Smith, Source Events

Steve Smith, Pride Flight 2018 (formerly with Florida Keys & Key West)

Shannon Spillett, Kimpton Hotels & Restaurants

Rick Stiffler, Preferred Hotels

Alessio Virgili, Quiiky Viaggi

Srimala Waraphaskul, Tourism Authority of Thailand

Bob Witeck, Witeck Communications, Inc.

CONTENTS

FIGURES

(following page 90)

Figure 1. Visit Britain extends an invitation to gay men.

Figure 2. Visit Britain offers an invitation to lesbians.

Figure 3. Fort Lauderdale markets the best of the destination.

Figure 4. Saying "I do" in Las Vegas.

Figure 5. Fort Lauderdale uses real lesbians in its ads.

Figure 6. Stockholm's Leading Ladies campaign.

Figure 7. Fort Lauderdale courts the trans traveler.

Figure 8. GayGermany—100% so you.

Figure 9. Pink Pillow Berlin Collection.

Figure 10. Borgata boasts its 100% score on the Corporate Equality Index.

Figure 11. United Airlines: Openly and proudly LGBT-friendly.

Figure 12. It all starts in DC.

Figure 13. Tel Aviv gay vibe.

Figure 14. Azamara Club Cruises uses an LGBT booking code.

Figure 15. Alaska Airlines is "calling all explorers."

Figure 16. The Porter Airlines mascot.

Figure 17. Marriott Hotels: #LoveTravels.

Figure 18. Luxor Las Vegas appeals to the upscale traveler.

Figure 19. Preferred Hotels offers an upscale LGBT experience.

Figure 20. Thailand: "Go Thai, Be Free."

Figure 21. Brazil's National Family Day.

Figure 22. ITB's Gay & Lesbian Travel Pavilion: Long Live Diversity!

ACKNOWLEDGMENTS

We wish to thank Bill Cohen, who cofounded Haworth Press and is publisher at Harrington Park Press. We also wish to thank Bill's exceptional team: Steven Rigolosi, the book development editor; Patrick Ciano, the book designer; Ann Twombly, our copy editor; and Columbia University Press. We are grateful to Bill and the entire team for this opportunity and for their assistance every step of the way. It is a privilege to work with them.

We want to thank everyone who generously gave their time and expertise captured in this book.

JEFF: I would like to acknowledge God for all of the gifts in my life; my partner, Todd Mckee, for his patience and love; my mother, Lucille Guaracino; my ABB, Ed Salvato; my friends Bruce Yelk, Kevin Hanaway, Joanne Calabria, Meryl Levitz, Marcia and Benjamin Gelbart, and Mark Segal; my family, Jerry, Kim, Taylor, Travis, Ava, and Luke; my aunts, uncles, and cousins; Dr. Brian Little; Tom Roth and David Paisely; Philadelphia Gay Tourism Caucus; the staff and board at Visit Philadelphia (Angela Val, Cara Schneider, and Cathy McVey); the staff and board at the Atlantic City Alliance (Liz Cartmell, Dave Wadell, Judi Ludovico, Christine Spencer, Francine Palumbo, and Kellianne Nicholas); my colleagues and friends Charlie Rounds, Andrew Davis, Susan Hamilton, Andi Coyle, Linda Sonnie, Sabrina Tamburino-Thorn, Nicole Cashman, Sandy Hillman, Liz Feldman, Melanie Sole, Rosalyn McPherson, Gregg Kaminski and Dan MacDonald, Don Guardian, Gary Hill and John Schultz, and Laura Burkhardt; the staff and board of Welcome America, Inc., especially Mayor Jim Kenney, the Altus Agency, and very particularly all of my dear friends in Philadelphia, Atlantic City, and the world, who are too many to name but you are in my heart.

ED: I would like to acknowledge my family, Anthony, Elaine, John, Steve, Teresa, Annette, Mike, and their families, and special acknowledgment to Sue Childs, my late sister-in-law, who was always supportive. I'd also like to acknowledge Billy Kolber and David Alport, founders of *Out&About* and my original gay travel mentors; Barbara Kolber, who has kept my i's dotted and t's crossed through two travel magazines; my supportive friends Konstantinos Sarvanakis, Mary P. Keating, Linda Adams, Eric Schultz, Steve Amsden, Evan Frank, Chris Cooper, Dave Zebny, Stephanie La Tour, Jeanne Reid, and Lori Goldstein; and Jeff Guaracino, my ABB.

And we wish to acknowledge everyone who participated in small and big ways to help shape the book.

—Jeff Guaracino
Philadelphia

—Ed Salvato
New York City

MILESTONES IN LGBT HISTORY, TOURISM, AND MARKETING

	1958	1960–1969	1970–1973	1974–1979	1980–1983	1983
PUBLICATIONS	*Le Guide Gris/ The Gray Guide* First travel guide written for gay male travelers	**1964** *The Damron Guide* Bob Damron launches travel guide for gay men	**1970** *Spartacus* (UK/International) first published	**1974** *Lesbian Connection* launched Published monthly and distributed free; the longest-running lesbian publication **1974** *Girls Guide to International Living* First travel guide specifically for the lesbian traveler (became *The Gaia Guide* in 1975)		*Ferrari Guides: Women's Travel in Your Pocket*
HISTORY, EVENTS, AND DEMONSTRATIONS		**1960s** First U.S. LGBT demonstrations in Philadelphia and Washington, D.C.	**1970s** Pride marches launched in New York, San Francisco, Chicago, and Los Angeles **1970s** More than 100 women's music festivals are held across the United States and Western Europe, including Womyn's Music Festival (1976–2015)	**1974** Masks Parade: First demonstration in Israel by gays and lesbians **1976** Red Party launched in Columbus, Ohio	**1982** Gay Games launched in San Francisco	Folsom Street Fair launched in San Francisco

1985–1986	1987–1989	1990–1991	1992–1993	1994–1999	2000–2005	2006–2015
	1989 *Damron Guide: The Women's Traveller*	**1990s** Traditional travel guides publish LGBT content in their directories	**1992** *Out&About* First travel newsletter for gay men	**1995** Utopia Asia launched First gay-travel website in English for Asian destinations (also in print format) *Fodor's* publishes its first LGBT travel guide	**2003** *Out Traveler* magazine launches	
1985 White Party launched in Miami	**1987** The Homomonument The Netherlands hosts the first monument commemorating all gays and lesbians subjected to persecution because of their homosexuality	**1991** First Dyke March in San Francisco **1991** Dinah Shore Weekend launched **1991** Black and Blue Party launched in Montreal	**1993** American Airlines adds sexual orientation to its nondiscrimination policy	**1994** GLEAM forms (American Airlines' corporate-sponsored gay employee resource group) **1994** Community Marketing Tom Roth produces the first LGBT tourism research study	**2000** American Airlines extends equal partner benefits to same-sex couples **2001** First legal same-sex marriages in the Netherlands help launch gay honeymoon travel **2003** Taipei hosts first Taiwan Pride	**2006** Out Games launched in Montreal **2006** São Paolo Gay Pride recognized **2015** Same-sex marriage legalized in the United States

For a list of recommended books about the international LGBT travel market, see sections 6E and 6F (Further Reading and Annotated Bibliography).

MILESTONES IN LGBT HISTORY, TOURISM, AND MARKETING

	1958	1960–1969	1970–1973	1974–1979	1980–1983	1983
TRAVEL AND ACCOMMODATIONS			**1973** Hans Ebensten, the "Father of Gay Travel," launches the first gay tour company	**1976** Island House Key West opens (world's first gay guesthouse) **1977** Lima Tours (first gay tours to Peru)		
MARKETING			**1970's** Islanders Travel is the first company to use the words "Gay Travel" in a paid display ad in the *New York Times*	**1977** Provincetown, Mass., begins marketing to LGBT visitors **1978** Key West Business Guild formed to market the Conch Republic	**1983** IGLTA founded with 25 travel agents and hoteliers	

1985–1986	1987–1989	1990–1991	1992–1993	1994–1999	2000–2005	2006–2015
1986 RSVP Vacations, "A Cruise to Remember" Cruise provides a safe vacation environment for gay men and lesbians		**1990s** Lesbian travel companies begin: Olivia Cruises, French Escapes, Walking Women Holidays, Sappho Travel **1990s** Bear events spread globally **1991** Atlantis Events hosts its first all-gay resort event	**1992** Royal Palms Fort Lauderdale (luxurious small lodging for gay men only)		**2003** Axel Hotels, first gay hotel chain, opens in Barcelona **2004** R Family Vacations launched	
			1993 Travel+Leisure and Condé Nast Traveler use the word *gay* for the first time	**1994** Tourism Montreal begins large outreach to gay and lesbian market	**2000** British Tourism Authority launches LGBT marketing campaign **2002** Orbitz is first online travel site to launch LGBT section **2004** Philadelphia produces the first TV commercial targeted at the LGBT travel market	**2010** IGLTA becomes first gay organization affiliated with UNWTO **2014** Greater Fort Lauderdale CVB launches groundbreaking trans travel initiative **2016** Fort Lauderdale expands LGBT family initiative

FOREWORD

Worldwide travel is not compulsory. Great minds have been fostered entirely by staying close to home. Moses never got further than the Promised Land. Da Vinci and Beethoven never left Europe. Shakespeare hardly went anywhere at all—certainly not to Elsinore or the coast of Bohemia.
—Jan Morris

Jan Morris, one of the world's great minds, beloved writers, and avid travelers, is right. For many of us, travel is not required. For lesbians and gay men, bisexuals and transgender people, however, it surely is a powerful impulse, even a need.

Jan Morris also made her journey from one gender to another and never seemed to fear an obstacle in her path. LGBT travelers can benefit from her example. And so will readers of this *Handbook of LGBT Tourism and Hospitality*.

Nearly twenty-five years ago, I began advising business leaders about the economic contributions of gay men and lesbians (and soon thereafter, transgender people and bisexuals). Back then, it was not so puzzling why major brands were shy about marketing to these consumers. Many saw the proposition as an honest calculation of risk versus reward. Years ago, one destination marketer asked me whether, by attracting one gay tourist, he might repel two or three other straight visitors.

Gay people understand that we're not always made to feel welcome. The world has not always been very welcoming to the "few," the "outsiders," and the "different." Nonetheless, that knowledge can be liberating. When LGBT people recognize that the world isn't going to change us, we think: Why not change the world instead? Even if just one person at a time, one brand at a time, or one destination at a time?

This mind-set is exactly why the travel and hospitality industry leads the business world today by showing how to welcome all of us. For a quarter century, I've had the privilege to work with some of the best of the best, including American Airlines and Marriott, and I've observed the pioneering work of many top brands at home and around the world. There is no longer debate that the world of travel is about welcome and respect—for all.

It's easy to see why. Contemporary hospitality brands know that they face fierce competition for every talent, for every guest, for every experience. We have transformed the LGBT community's increased visibility and solid market data into a compelling business case that no travel leader can ignore. And now, as businesses increasingly seek to market to millennials, we see that LGBT inclusion and awareness is a priority for new generations, too.

Luckily for us all, Jeff Guaracino and Ed Salvato are the ideal navigators for this rewarding journey. Their combined years of marketing savvy and leadership—and their unparalleled network of travel experts, writers, researchers, marketers, and sales leaders—have delivered a road map to help businesses navigate all aspects of LGBT tourism and hospitality marketing in the coming years. You hold that road map in your hands now.

Shakespeare never roamed far, as Jan Morris reminds us. Books, however, can truly transport us—and I promise you that this book will do exactly that.

Bob Witeck
Witeck Communications, Inc.
Washington, D.C.

Authors' note: *Witeck Communications provides strategic public relations and marketing communications services for corporate and nonprofit clients who believe, as we do, that protecting and enhancing their reputations are key to their success. Witeck's work and clients often focus on social and market issues and how they influence corporations, nonprofits, foundations, and government agencies.*

INTRODUCTION

This book is about smart business. It is about expanding your travel and hospitality business through the simple and elegant power of the invitation: a sincere invitation to LGBT (lesbian, gay, bisexual, and transgender) travelers to discover your travel product (see Figures 1 and 2). This book will give you the tools you need to build an authentic and effective marketing program for the worldwide LGBT market segment.

Handbook of LGBT Tourism and Hospitality is a guide to success for hospitality professionals, teachers, students, marketing and sales professionals, travel agents, tour operators, destination marketing organizations, trade associations, meeting planners, consultants, marketing and communications professionals, convention and visitors bureaus, governments, media, researchers, and sales teams from hotels, cruise lines, airlines, and tour operators.

Nearly all businesses have LGBT customers, whether they are acknowledged or not. Some businesses may be starting out, just thinking about whether, why, and how to market to LGBT travelers. Other businesses already in the market may be seeking to increase their market share or to get more customers by enhancing their marketing outreach to LGBT travelers. Whether you are new or experienced, this book presents the data, case studies, and tips from experienced professionals that you need to expand your business.

Handbook of LGBT Tourism and Hospitality is designed as an easy-to-read, practical, and relevant guidebook to assist your marketing efforts in the increasingly competitive global travel and hospitality industry. We hope that industry professionals, educators, and students will use this book as a resource to learn about the market, develop strategies, and build effective campaigns. This book touches on LGBT travel history, but it is not a history book. Rather, it is a handbook for all who are interested in the LGBT tourism and hospitality industry. At its core is the belief that LGBT tourism is about good business.

To provide the best practical advice for marketing to the LGBT segment, the book provides a number of useful features.

Q&A with industry leaders

As part of our research, we interviewed eighty-five industry leaders. We combined their insights (along with the insights of many other tourism and hospitality professionals) with our experience in the world of LGBT travel to provide a "real world" look at best practices. Throughout this handbook you will find original, never-before-published interviews with experts in the field—some of whom have made history in the LGBT travel segment and who have shaped the contours of this evolving market segment. These interviews provide insight into not only marketing strategy, but also business return on investment (ROI).

Case studies and company spotlights

Throughout the text we provide case studies with specific examples from nearly every aspect of the tourism and hospitality industry. As some of the case studies show, LGBT tourism still can be controversial and a "hard sell" in the boardroom or to elected officials. The case studies will help you navigate through controversies by helping you build your business case with research and empirical data. Company spotlights shine light on businesses that have been particularly innovative or successful in reaching LGBT travelers.

Best practices and expert tips

No two travel products or destinations are the same. The best practices and expert tips sprinkled throughout the book will help you customize your own LGBT tourism marketing effort and help you understand this evolving and growing segment. You can use these tips to build a successful marketing campaign for your destination, product, or service.

International perspectives

Of course, the LGBT travel market is not limited to U.S. domestic travel. Chapter 5 of this handbook looks at LGBT travel professionals around the world. Throughout the book, "International Perspective" features offer insights into different countries' and cultures' approaches to welcoming LGBT travelers. An auto loan that makes your dream car a reality patrick

Educator's discussion guide

Handbook of LGBT Tourism and Hospitality includes an educator's discussion guide developed by Michael F. Sheridan. Each chapter concludes with discussion questions, and additional information is available online at www.LGBTexpert.com. Sheridan serves as a program director and full-time faculty member of the Temple University School of Sport, Tourism and Hospitality Management in Philadelphia.

Though we wrote this book as an easy-to-use handbook that helps you find information quickly and easily, we recommend that you read the time line and Chapter 1 for the industry context that they provide. Then dive deeper into the different topics by exploring other chapters.

Safe travels.

1

THE FOUNDATIONS OF
LGBT TOURISM AND HOSPITALITY

CHAPTER SUMMARY

This chapter covers the following foundations of LGBT tourism and hospitality: your "elevator pitch": the importance of developing a specific program for LGBT tourism; sizing the LGBT segment: buying power; the importance of the LGBT segment in the travel industry; tips before launching your LGBT marketing campaign; success in the LGBT travel market: and top ten tips from Jeff and Ed.

KEY TERMS

power of the invitation
homophobia
anti-gay laws
LGBT marketing
Corporate Equality Index
SCRUFF
Grindr
LGBT travel spending
LGBT destinations
Community Marketing & Insights (CMI)
International Gay & Lesbian Travel
    Association (IGLTA)
Gay Pride

Guaracino, Jeff, and Salvato, Ed, *Handbook of LGBT Tourism and Hospitality*
dx.doi.org/10.17312/harringtonparkpress/2017.03.hlgbtth.001
© 2017 by Jeff Guaracino and Ed Salvato

1A | YOUR "ELEVATOR PITCH": THE IMPORTANCE OF DEVELOPING A SEGMENT-SPECIFIC PROGRAM FOR LGBT TOURISM

Your colleagues, boss, board, your straight or LGBT family or friends—whether inside or outside the travel industry—may ask: "Why do we need to specifically target LGBT travelers? Have we not moved beyond the 'gay ghetto'?" Our experience and our interviews with international tourism professionals indicate that a specific, sustained, and smart LGBT tourism program is needed more than ever. Here is your "elevator pitch" for an LGBT tourism campaign.

1. There is nothing more powerful than an invitation. Not every community, country, or business welcomes LGBT travelers. Among the hundreds of global destinations that are looking for new visitors, relatively few actively reach out to LGBT travelers. LGBT consumers don't necessarily assume that they are welcome at a particular destination, or they might not know which destinations would interest them. A specific campaign reassures the traveler, and it gives you a competitive edge. It also sends a signal to the friends, families, and allies of the LGBT segment that you are gay welcoming, and it has increasingly become a marker and motivator for straight millennial travelers that you're a hip and forward-looking destination, hotel, or cruise line.

2. Homophobia still exists today—the tourism and hospitality industries can combat it. In LGBT-progressive cities, countries, and companies, marketers can easily fall into the trap of believing that homophobia has disappeared. Like ageism, racism, and sexism, however, homophobia seems to be baked into humans culturally. In fact, in many countries, LGBT persons can be persecuted and killed with impunity. In recent years, ISIS has hurled gay men off roofs and stoned them to death.[1] Troubling reports of homophobic harassment, threats, and violence persist even in gay-popular destinations like Amsterdam, London, New York City, and San Francisco. Even in the world's most tolerant places, including the Scandinavian countries that passed laws protecting gay men and lesbians decades ago, homophobia and transphobia can still lurk beneath the surface. In August 2015 *Time* magazine ran the headline "Why Transgender People Are Being Murdered at a Historic Rate" with an accompanying story about transgender crimes in the United States.[2]

Consider these other disturbing examples from the international press:

- In November 2011 the United Nations reported that at least seventy-six countries retain laws that criminalize people on the basis of their sexual orientation and gender identity or expression, including laws criminalizing consensual same-sex relationships among adults.[3]

Meryl Levitz, president and CEO of Visit Philadelphia, explains the power of the invitation perfectly: "Marketers must not forget that people want to be invited. People need to be invited and you do that by choosing imagery that they know is for them, placing it in media that is for them and making a promise of what people can expect all the way through the travel experience. For gay and lesbian travelers who aren't sure if they are going to be welcomed for who they are, an invitation is definitely needed."[*]

Visit Philadelphia devotes significant resources to create a genuine invitation to LGBT travelers to visit the city. It integrates inclusive imagery throughout its website, incorporating LGBT people within "mainstream" images. In addition, its robust and regularly updated LGBT microsite includes stories, pictures, and videos that speak directly to potential gay and lesbian visitors, which translate into a global twenty-four-hour "you are welcome" sign pointing toward the City of Brotherly Love.

Nikki Grossman, president of the Greater Fort Lauderdale Convention and Visitors Bureau, says that without a specific campaign, "the expression of welcome for gay travelers wouldn't be known. If you want someone to know something about your destination, you have to really put it out there, you have to let them know who you are, what you are thinking and what you have to offer, how they will be treated as a visitor, and so you need that campaign. Even though Fort Lauderdale was early, we needed that first campaign to just say 'Hi' and 'Here we are.' Now our campaign is 'Hi, here we are and this is why you should choose us over a number of competitors.' You've got to have a gay campaign; otherwise, gay travelers will be lured to another destination."[†] (See Figure 3.)

Because of its open invitation, Fort Lauderdale is a top destination for LGBT travelers and home to the greatest number of same-sex couples in the country. The Greater Fort Lauderdale Convention and Visitors Authority calls the city the "Gay Capital of the United States" and proudly promotes its rank as the country's seventh-most popular LGBT travel destination. The city welcomed a record-breaking 1.3 million LGBT visitors in 2013. These visitors represented 10 percent of all visitors to the city and spent $1.48 billion, or 14 percent of the city's overall revenue of $10.6 billion.[‡]

[*] Jeff Guaracino, *Gay and Lesbian Tourism: The Essential Guide for Marketing* (Boston: Elsevier, 2007), 5–6.

[†] Interview with Nikki Grossman, August 11, 2015.

[‡] Greater Fort Lauderdale Hello Sunny, "Greater Fort Lauderdale Gives 10.6 Billion 'Thank Yous' on National Tourism Appreciation Day," May 8, 2014, www.sunny.org/press-releases/post/greater-fort-lauderdale-gives -106-billion-thank-yous-on-national-tourism-appreciation-day/.

- Russia is reversing its liberal approach to the LGBT community and sending more Russians back into the closet. Consider this account by the conservative news network Al-Jazeera from September 2015:

  > Activists say it has fuelled anti-gay abuse, discrimination, and violence, spawned a "chilling effect," and victimized young lesbian, gay, bisexual, and transgender (LGBT) people and deterred them from coming out and seeking support.
  >
  > The Russian legislation banned the spreading of "propaganda for non-traditional sexual relations" to minors and introduced fines for individuals and organizations that breach the law, which critics describe as arbitrary and hard to implement.
  >
  > The law is seen by many as one in a series of moves by President Vladimir Putin to crack down on dissent, smother civil society, and draw closer to the Russian Orthodox Church, which has spoken out against homosexuality and is one of the most influential institutions in the country.[4]

- The same day as the New York Pride Parade on Sunday, June 28, 2015, Reuters reported, "Turkish police fired water cannon and rubber pellets to disperse a Gay Pride parade in central Istanbul on Sunday, after organisers said they had been refused permission to march this year because of the Muslim holy month of Ramadan."[5]

- The *Las Vegas Sun* reported on April 27, 2011, that the swanky Cosmopolitan of Las Vegas resort encountered a transgender issue with a guest. The report said that a "guest . . . identified as a 'pre-op trans' named Stephanie, said upon leaving the women's room she was taken out of the resort by security guards, told she was trespassing on Cosmopolitan property and she would be arrested if she didn't leave. She said she was photographed and told she was banned from returning to the hotel."[6] In response to the incident, the hotel issued the following statement:

  > The Cosmopolitan of Las Vegas is committed to maintaining a community that recognizes and values the inherent dignity of every person, by fostering sensitivity, understanding and mutual respect of our guests and employees. We sincerely regret any misunderstanding or inappropriate actions that any member of our staff may have taken. And to ensure increased sensitivity within this area, the organization will focus on continued training and ongoing awareness initiatives. In addition, we apologize to the individual guest and welcome her back to the resort anytime. Again, we would like to apologize to the LGBT community and anyone concerned and hope to demonstrate our firm dedication to fair and unbiased treatment of all.

  The statement takes responsibility for its role in the incident, but a much better option is to be more proactive about training staff in proper conduct and providing LGBT-friendly facilities.

- Barbados Minister of Tourism Richard Sealy rejects lesbian, gay, bisexual, and transgender tourism. Sealy, who is also chairman of the Caribbean Tourism Organization (CTO), admitted that while some destinations had taken a different approach in trying to tap into the lucrative LGBT market, he did not expect a similar approach in Barbados. Barbados's evangelical churches, Anglican clergy, and the Pentecostal Assemblies of the West Indies (PAWI) oppose LGBT tourism.[8]

Homophobia doesn't need to be horrific and obvious to be harmful. Sometimes all it takes is an arched eyebrow from the diners at another table for a traveler to release his partner's hand. In addition, lack of appropriate staff training or lack of attention to LGBT travelers' needs—for example, gender-neutral bathrooms—can make guests and staff uncomfortable or stir controversy.

In short, Safety and homophobia are legitimate concerns for all LGBT travelers. The U.S. Department of State recommends that LGBT citizens "avoid excessive physical displays of affection in public, particularly in more conservative countries or regions." Marketers need to be well aware of the laws and cultures of any particular destination.

LGBT travelers may find homophobia (expressed or latent) by travel suppliers or in their personal interactions with staff, locals, or other travelers throughout their trip. How should businesses respond to local homophobia? The answer is simple. Travel is about inviting people to visit your culture, your lives, and your place. LGBT travel is about safety, acceptance, and being who you are. Your goal is to welcome people who might not be out, accepted, or tolerated back home. Fostering an open dialogue on LGBT travel and the LGBT community will help you improve the visitor experience, as will providing reassurance that LGBT travelers are not only welcome but also safe.

TIPS FROM THE EXPERTS

CREATING A SAFE SPACE FOR IDENTITY AND SELF-EXPRESSION

Charlie Rounds is a pioneering LGBT travel professional and human rights activist. He has dedicated his entire career to ensuring equal rights for all people and to advancing LGBT equality through travel. Rounds believes that LGBT travel can be transformative to the global human experience and that more than ever LGBT people around the world are looking for an LGBT travel experience. In short, the future of LGBT travel is big, bright, and necessary. According to Rounds, developed countries like the United States, Great Britain, and Canada are now beacons to the LGBT community worldwide, communicating that equality, acceptance, and inclusion are possible.[*]

Rounds believes that LGBT travel is about safety and identity expression. Even in the United States, Rounds says, 99 percent of people are uncomfortable with a public display of same-sex affection. For these reasons, effective LGBT tourism ads often promote the intimacy, safety, and freedom of the experience. For example, gay cruise charters such as Atlantis Events, RSVP Vacations, Olivia, Source Events, and Brand G Vacations create a safe, open environment that appeals to LGBT travelers from all over the world. Many of these LGBT travelers are persecuted culturally, religiously, or legally in their home countries. As examples, he cites wealthy Middle Eastern LGBT persons, newly liberated LGBT refugees pouring out of Europe, and LGBT persons in Ukraine or Moldova.

[*] Interview with Charlie Rounds, October 28, 2015.

3. LGBT marketing is about knowing your customer and yourself. The LGBT market is no less segmented than any other market. Despite the common use of *LGBT* as an umbrella term, wide variations exist within each part of the LGBT community. For example, LGBT travelers may be in or out of the closet, and their travel experience can be shaped by their culture, gender, age, religion, whether they have children, the laws relating to homosexuality at home, and many other factors.

LGBT marketing is also about knowing your company, your destination, and your travel product's relationship to the LGBT community. Chapter 2 dives deeply into knowing your customer, so here let's focus on knowing yourself and your company.

Surveys show that LGBT consumers prefer to buy from gay-friendly companies. Thus, telling your story gives you a competitive advantage with these consumers. So align your business with what is important to the LGBT community, and shout it from the rooftops!

Many LGBT people evaluate tourism and hospitality businesses on the basis not just of their treatment of LGBT travelers, but also of their treatment of LGBT employees. Orbitz Worldwide, Marriott, American Airlines, Delta Airlines, IBM, AT&T, Comcast NBC Universal, and Coca-Cola are widely recognized as embracing diversity in their corporate policies. Proud of their commitment to diversity, these companies often broadcast their support of their LGBT employees in marketing programs and employee resource groups.

One measure of how well LGBT employees are treated in the corporate world is the Human Rights Campaign Foundation's Corporate Equality Index (CEI), a benchmarking tool focused on U.S. corporate policies and practices pertinent to lesbian, gay, bisexual, and transgender employees. In the 2015 CEI report, 366 major businesses—comprising nearly every industry and location in the United States—earned a top score of 100 percent and the distinction of "Best Places to Work for LGBT Equality."

Some corporations, however, still have a long way to go. As the *New York Times* reported on July 1, 2015: "In the Human Rights Campaign's most recent Corporate Equality Index . . . Exxon again ranked last, with a score of minus 25—the only company ever to have received a negative score. After Exxon acquired Mobil in 1999, Exxon rescinded Mobil's policies prohibiting discrimination on the basis of sexual orientation and ended its policy of providing benefits to same-sex partners. Many gay and lesbian drivers have boycotted Exxon service stations ever since."[9]

In more countries, data support the idea that a "tipping point" has been passed and businesses now have more to gain than lose by being seen as consistent supporters of their LGBT customers and employees.[10] Now is the right time to begin or expand your LGBT marketing effort.

4. Relationship marketing and customer retention are the marketer's ultimate goals. Many companies see relationship marketing as their ultimate goal. Relationship marketing focuses on customer satisfaction and retention rather than simple sales transactions. The underlying belief, supported by the data, is that retaining current customers is much more cost-effective than finding new ones. Relationship marketing focuses not on wide-blast e-mails and sales campaigns (though such techniques are still used) but, rather, on a personal relationship between the company and its customers. Jon Allen, proprietor of one of the world's most famous—perhaps *the* most famous—gay men's guesthouses in Key West, Florida, may have said it best: "Effective marketing is just telling the truth in a way that gets people's attention."

How do you increase your commitment to relationship marketing? Start by telling your company's story. Then personalize the message to the individual customer to craft an authentic invitation.

Remember that LGBT travelers seek specific travel experiences or products with an understanding of their culture, history, community, world perspective, and desires. Relationship marketing starts with knowing your customer. The next step is customizing your company's messages and images to make them resonate with the LGBT community, and then to disseminate this customized content through social media, advertising, and other marketing channels.

During a Source Events cruise visiting Italy, Croatia, and Montenegro, we conducted a focus group with over a dozen experienced world travelers. We asked them: "What makes you buy a gay travel product?" On this cruise, a cabin ranged from $5,000 to $14,000. We met quite a few well-to-do gay men from around the world who chose to purchase a gay vacation. Why would a group of gay men choose to sail on the *Royal Clipper* (part of the Star Clipper Cruise Line) and pay more per cabin than

BEST PRACTICES

KNOWING YOUR CUSTOMERS AND CUSTOMIZING YOUR PRODUCTS

LGBT travelers are just like other travelers: they want to be respected and they want a meaningful travel experience. Respect can be as simple as recognizing that two men checking into a hotel room may want to share one bed.

In other cases, travelers may respond well to a program tailored specifically for them. For example, R Family Vacations pairs family-friendly travel experiences with ancillary programming of interest to multigenerational LGBT families.

The *New York Times* travel writer Steven McElroy profiled Atlantis Events, the world's most successful tour operator for the gay and lesbian travel segment. Brian J. Nash, an Atlantis entertainer, described the uniqueness of gay travel on a fully chartered cruise ship as follows: "I think no matter how socially acceptable being gay becomes, and thank God it's continually getting better, there's something about being on this magical island where everyone is like you and you can be entirely yourself and be as ridiculous as you want to be or as romantic and loving in public as you want to be. There's a comfort level, there's no looking over one's shoulder."

they would any other week of the year? Most of them talked about the sense of community they found on board. One respondent, a successful entrepreneur, said that he and his husband are so busy in their day-to-day lives that they have no time to make friends. On Source Events cruises, they have made friends for life, friends whom they see on subsequent Source Events cruises. On this trip, these gay men said, they felt safe and free to be themselves while exploring remote corners of the world (the Balkans, Tahiti, South Africa) and not visiting the same gay resort areas over and over again.

1B | SIZING THE LGBT SEGMENT: BUYING POWER

Estimates of the size of the LGBT segment of the travel market vary from study to study, and many researchers question the accuracy of these numbers because of the research methodology (self-selected versus randomized polling) and other flaws. Overall, though, many studies estimate similar levels of spending and buying power within the segment, and these levels have remained mostly consistent over time.

OVERALL LGBT MARKET SIZE AND CONSUMER SPENDING POWER IN THE UNITED STATES

It is very difficult to estimate the number of LGBT travelers in any given year. To date, there has been no comprehensive way of counting every LGBT traveler. Industry professionals cannot identify LGBT travelers simply by using their eyes, as they can with, say, male, female, black, Latino, Asian, or Caucasian travelers. In other words, unless a company specifically tracks LGBT customers (perhaps through a loyalty program or e-mail profiles), LGBT travelers can be "invisible." That said, the industry is starting to get a better sense of the numbers through technology, research, and government agencies. For example:

- Facebook allows users to self-identify as LGBT.
- SCRUFF and Grindr include millions of self-identified gay male app users.
- More research studies ask questions about sexual orientation and identity.
- The U.S. Census tracks same-sex households.

As technology and research improve our ability to track same-sex households, sexual orientation, and gender identity in surveys, we can expect to see better data over time. In the meantime, one respected financial firm, LGBT Capital, estimated in 2015 that the global spending power of the LGBT consumer segment is $3.7 trillion per year; the LGBT population was estimated at about 450 million.[11]

Another estimate of market size comes from Gary J. Gates, the Williams Distinguished Scholar at the Williams Institute at the UCLA School of Law and a coauthor of *The Gay and Lesbian Atlas* (Urban Institute Press, 2004). Gates wrote in the *Washington Post* in April 2011: "I recently reviewed findings from 11 large surveys conducted since 2004, seven in the United States and four internationally. Averaging across the U.S.-based surveys, I found that nearly 9 million Americans (3.8 percent of adults) self-identify as LGBT. That's equivalent to the population of New Jersey. An estimated 19 million Americans (8.2 percent) report having engaged in some same-sex sexual behavior, and nearly 26 million (11 percent) report some same-sex sexual attraction. The latter figure is equivalent to the population of Texas."[12]

GLOBAL ESTIMATES OF LGBT TRAVEL SPENDING

Out Now Consulting, based in the Netherlands, predicted that the global potential value of the lesbian, gay, bisexual, and transgender leisure travel market in 2015 would reach a record $200 billion. Out Now based its estimate on the innovative and groundbreaking LGBT 2030 research program, which measures LGBT consumer spending, purchasing habits, and brand preferences in twenty-four countries.

LGBT 2030 indicates that in the United States gay travelers spend $52.3 billion per year. The next-largest country in gay travel spending is Brazil, at $22.9 billion. European countries combined account for $58.3 billion. In Canada, Travel Gay Canada estimates LGBT Canadian travel spending at $7 billion annually.

Gay and lesbian visitors contribute about $6.8 billion to the Spanish economy, edging out France as Europe's top LGBT destination, according to a report by LGBT Capital. According to Spanish government estimates, gay people spend about 30 percent more on average than mainstream tourists in Spain, boosting an economy where tourism accounts for 12 percent of jobs.[13]

Asian LGBT travel is fast developing; LGBT travel spending in Asia is estimated at over $1 trillion, and China alone is estimated to have an LGBT population of more than 80 million.

In Chapters 2 and 3 of this handbook, we summarize the economic size of micro-markets in travel, including the lesbian market (section 2B), family market (section 2E), trans market (section 2D), and sporting events market (section 3C).

1C | THE IMPORTANCE OF THE LGBT SEGMENT IN THE TRAVEL INDUSTRY

LGBT travel is increasingly understood as a segment in which more and "new" money can be made. LGBT travel started as small-group travel and leisure travel. Today the segment has grown more mature, and it now has a firm footing in the SMERF (social, military, education, religious, and fraternal) market, along with many new opportunities, such as weddings and honeymoons (see Figure 4). The meeting and group market continues to expand as smaller meetings (such as the Out & Equal Conference) grow larger and more lucrative, and as sporting events (such as the World Out Games) gain in popularity.

Community Marketing & Insights, an authoritative research and marketing firm based in San Francisco, believes that the LGBT market receives a great deal of attention among businesspeople for a number of reasons:

- Many LGBT couples are DINKs—"Dual Income, No Kids." That situation could be slowly changing, however, as millennials age into their child-rearing years.

- Many LGBT people like to travel as part of their cultural identity.

- There is the perception (not necessarily accurate) of greater income and wealth among LGBT people.

- LGBT people can be reached with targeted outreach opportunities.

- Many LGBT people are exceptionally loyal to specific brands and destinations.

- Although LGBT people make up only about 3–6 percent of the adult population, surveys show that they travel nearly twice as much as the average American.

1D | TIPS BEFORE LAUNCHING YOUR LGBT MARKETING CAMPAIGN

Maybe you have not yet started your LGBT marketing campaign. You're not alone. Every one of the eighty-five leaders in the global LGBT travel and hospitality industries that we interviewed for this book started in the same place: the beginning.

Martine Ainsworth-Wells is the director of marketing communications and commerce for the European Tourism Association (ETOA) and former director of marketing and communications for Visit London, the official promotional organization for London. As an out, proud heterosexual travel executive who launched London's LGBT tourism marketing campaign and attracted global events, including World Pride 2012, Ainsworth-Wells offers these six tips for launching your LGBT marketing campaign:

1. Make the decision: Are you an LGBT destination? If you can't stand up enthusiastically and be counted, don't go there yet. Wait until you are ready, or wait until you can easily demonstrate your enthusiasm. You can't fake it. You will be competing against destinations like London, Berlin, New York, San Francisco, and Bangkok, which have very strong credentials in this area.

2. Jump in. Don't dip your toes in the water; rather, jump in. This is what Martine did: "I'm a straight woman and never worked in LGBT marketing before. I was challenged by the mayor of London, Ken Livingston, and the Visit London leadership team to engage everyone. So I just jumped in."

3. Employ experts. You will make mistakes. You don't want to but you will. Accept these mistakes and learn from them. As Martine says, "I joined the mayor's office's working group on diversity. I never felt excluded. Experts allowed me to learn, grow, and develop."

4. Don't make it niche. (This is an unusual statement.) No LGBT campaign can be successful when straight people market to LGBT people. Bring people and teams together and create cooperation among them.

5. Engage in the community. Ask yourself: "Where do I need to be? Whom do I need to speak to? Where do I need to position myself?" Martine describes her experience: "I joined the International Gay and Lesbian Travel Association (IGLTA). I attended Community Marketing & Insights' annual conference on international tourism. I attended Pride parades. I wanted to really understand the community. I walked the walk. I saw, experienced, and did more than most straight women would have, but I wanted to immerse myself."

6. Don't forget the L, B, and T. When you are presenting content for the LGBT market, be careful not to focus exclusively on the gay male market. There are many oportunities out there, among them marriages, meetings and conventions, and LGBT sporting competitions.

TIPS FROM THE EXPERTS

KEEPING THE L, B, AND T IN LGBT

Tom Roth, founder and president of Community Marketing & Insights, cautions marketers: "There is no singular 'gay market' or even an 'LGBT market.' The LGBT community represents a 'slice' of the entire world population covering every interest, every culture, every profession, and more." Billy Kolber, cofounder of *ManAboutWorld* magazine, notes similarly, "There is a G, L, B, and T market, each of which has different behaviors, needs, motivations, and spending prowess." For more information:

- The lesbian market: section 2B
- The bisexual market: section 2C
- The trans market: section 2D

On the basis of our research and our experiences in the field, we offer ten key tips for success as you brainstorm, implement, and assess the effectiveness of LGBT business, marketing, or outreach.

1. Engage experts. The market, the culture, and the technology are moving quickly. Not only do you need to familiarize yourself with the LGBT market; you also need market knowledge quickly. Hire an expert. If you want to penetrate the Chinese market, for example, you'd hire someone from China who speaks Chinese fluently. The same is true in the LGBT space. There are smart, lean agencies and highly regarded industry experts who are passionate and deeply knowledgeable about the segment (see section 6A). Avoid imposters. Just being an LGBT person doesn't make that person an expert on the market. Avoid "me-search"—the opinions of one of your LGBT staff. That person can offer his or her own opinions but cannot speak for the entire LGBT community. Check out our website at www.LGBTexpert.com for a list of recommended agencies, consultants, and experts.

2. Compete for gay dollars. You need to be really smart with your marketing because others are eyeing your success and revenue. LGBT travelers have more travel choices, and with those options comes the need to reinvest in your LGBT customers to foster deep-rooted loyalty, garner repeat business, and keep top-of-mind awareness strong. Staying competitive with the LGBT segment requires fine-tuned research, a multiyear strategy, and dedicated budgets.

3. Approach LGBT marketing as hybrid international and multicultural marketing. LGBT marketing is increasingly a hybrid of multicultural and international marketing, moving away from a monolithic "diversity" market. In some ways the LGBT market is just as fragmented as many other markets. It mixes men and women, same- and opposite-sex attraction (in the case of bisexual travelers), gender identity, different consumer behaviors, different cultural identities and political perspectives, different history, different religious beliefs, and at times a different vernacular. Compare this situation to any foreign market. You market to cultural differences with an eye on the political, historical, and linguistic differences. You try to be sensitive and respectful, speak to experts (see tip 1 above), do your research, and execute a focused campaign. You should follow the same strategy with the LGBT market.

4. Expand your LGBT business by reaching out to multicultural and multigenerational markets. The most affluent gay men are over-targeted: everyone is going after this obvious market (composed of proudly out gay men with a lot of disposable income—the ones you see pictured in so much advertising). Smart marketers look at multicultural LGBT segments that are typically under-marketed to, including African Americans, Latinos, lesbians, and bisexuals. These travelers appreciate and respond to an authentic invitation, and they have money to spend.

5. Follow the gay market. Gay men are the original disrupters (a socially connected community forcing change at the grassroots level), early adopters of technology, and trendsetters. Grindr and SCRUFF arose before Tinder and undoubtedly inspired many copycats. As technology evolves and tracking becomes more precise, the gay male market can help marketers understand the future directions of other market segments.

6. Tailor your campaigns. Just throwing images of gay couples into mainstream media and creative (*creative* refers to any creative advertising or marketing communications) is not enough to build your brand or image with LGBT travelers. Rather, you need to focus on a specific, well-defined segment. By all means, maintain one overall campaign strategy, but also plan to execute a plan aimed at specific segments, like the LGBT segment and others. Technology can help you improve your efficiency, reach, and sales to your targeted customers.

7. Understand media consumption and buying. LGBT media consumption and media buying will continue to shift to the Internet and Internet-enabled mobile devices, but the power of local LGBT print media will continue to be a driving force for local market penetration. Sponsored news feeds and branded content online with a higher ability for sharing will continue to reach more people. LGBT editors and publishers of all kinds—both in print and online—will have an even stronger share of the voice. As local LGBT newspaper editorials, columns, and online news sites like Towleroad, *ManAboutWorld,* and platforms like Multimedia Platforms Inc. (a publicly traded LGBT media company) continue to grow, what the media say about you will matter even more.

8. Leverage technology. As technology continues to improve, marketers are increasingly able to measure the performance of their campaigns in all segments, including LGBT travelers. As consumers move to mobile and cross-platform media, the ability to market to and track consumers' behaviors and buying habits will improve even more. (See section 4 J for a case study explaining how Madonna helped sell her 2015–2016 "Rebel Heart" concert tour through Grindr, which was the best-selling platform for ticket sales for that concert.)[14]

9. Controversy pays! Certainly twenty years ago—and even five years ago—marketers may have feared launching an LGBT campaign or did so and dreaded backlash. Companies inside and outside the travel industry seem to benefit from anti-LGBT controversy from groups that have demonstrated no real power (for example, One Million

Moms' attack on Campbell's Soup). We don't recommend being controversial just for the sake of controversy, but if your message and your creative are authentic and you stand by that message, you will certainly weather and most likely benefit from controversy. For more information on navigating controversy, see section 3N.

10. Travel teaches other markets. The travel segment will be the model that other industries and governments follow to engage LGBT persons.

DISCUSSION QUESTIONS

1. Why do organizations need to specifically understand and reach out to LGBT travelers?
2. How have the changing attitudes toward and growing support for same-sex marriage (as well as laws that have legalized same-sex marriage) altered the efforts of travel marketers?
3. In what ways are marketers able to better track the estimated $3.7 trillion global spending power of the LGBT consumer segment?
4. Which factors affect the accuracy or dependability of the estimated spending power of the LGBT travel segment?
5. Thinking about your own job, company, business, or industry, which factors are the most important for you to consider before beginning an LBGT marketing campaign? Explain.

2

BUSINESS ESSENTIALS: UNDERSTANDING THE LGBT TRAVEL MARKET

CHAPTER SUMMARY

This chapter covers the following essential information about the LGBT travel market: understanding key segments and focusing your resources; lesbian travel; bisexual travel; putting the T in LGBT travel; LGBT family travel trends; the top ten trends in LGBT travel; and training, staff, business policies, and employee resource groups.

KEY TERMS

millennial LGBT travelers
same-sex marriages
same-sex honeymoons
five Ps of marketing
lesbian travel
bisexual travel
transgender travel
LGBT family travel
employee resource groups
LGBT business resource groups

Guaracino, Jeff, and Salvato, Ed, *Handbook of LGBT Tourism and Hospitality*
dx.doi.org/10.17312/harringtonparkpress/2017.03.hlgbtth.002
© 2017 by Jeff Guaracino and Ed Salvato

2A | UNDERSTANDING KEY SEGMENTS AND FOCUSING YOUR RESOURCES

The acronym LGBT encompasses an entire global community: lesbian, gay, bisexual, and transgender. Bottom lines improve as your business attracts and retains loyal customers with the right mix of travel products.

SEGMENTING THE MARKETS

Diving into data on the group represented by each letter is paramount in tourism marketing because not only are travelers L, G, B, or T, but they can also be black, European, American, or further identified under such categories as African American, Asian, married or single, young or old, parents of children or childless, and so on. Research conducted by Community Marketing & Insights has also uncovered generational differences, most notably between boomer and millennial LGBT travelers, especially in their attitudes, identities, and perceptions of the world. Some research has indicated that singling out millennials as "different" in some way may not be an effective strategy. Gen X or boomer LGBT travelers who have experienced discrimination throughout their lifetime, however, might want a specifically gay experience or demand to be recognized as an LGBT consumer or traveler. Fear of discrimination, politics, and household income play important roles in travel decisions by consumers across all age groups.

In short, LGBT travelers have as many dimensions as their heterosexual counterparts, in addition to the factor that comes with being LGBT. It's important to know the extent to which a consumer's sexuality or gender identity comes into play when he or she is making a purchase decision. For example, in deciding on the destination for a same-sex marriage and honeymoon, one's sexuality matters a great deal.

Same-sex marriages and honeymoons are clear-cut examples of travel based on sexuality. Not all travel situations are so unambiguous, however. A key question that marketers must answer is: When are travelers making decisions that are based on their sexuality and when are they making decisions in which sexuality does not play a role? For example, when is the trip just a business trip in which the LGBT traveler uses the corporate American Express Card and stays at a hotel chosen by the corporate office, and when is the traveler "buying gay" and paying for the LGBT travel experience?

Put simply, what is important in the travel experience for a gay man is not necessarily important for a lesbian or a transgender traveler. What points of distinction will give your travel product or marketing program an edge by tapping into the specific desires of the many LGBT travel segments?

One effective technique is to approach the LGBT travel segments as you would an international or new market segment. What is the traveler's history, worldview, religious affiliation, culture, or political standing in a particular country? For example, an LGBT traveler in the United States, Canada, or Great Britain might have a worldview that is very different from that of an LGBT traveler in China, Africa, or the Middle East.

Because every business works within a budget, one of your key aims should be to focus your resources in a way that gets the most bang for the buck. How do you decide where to focus? The answer depends on which segment you are interested in marketing to and what your product can offer. Answer the five Ps of marketing (product, place, price, promotion, and packaging) to match your offerings to your ideal customers. For example, Source Events (a luxury group tour operator) markets to wealthy gay men with high household incomes living in urban settings with no children in the household. R Family Vacations focuses on LGBT family travel, offering trips that accommodate children's school schedules. If lesbians are the focus, women's events can be a draw.

MARKET RESEARCH RESOURCES

To help you build your marketing plan, you might turn to some of the world's foremost authorities on global LGBT tourism and consumer research. Among the best-known are:

- Community Marketing & Insights (California)
- Out Now Consulting (the Netherlands)
- The Williams Institute (California)
- Witeck Communications with Package Facts, a division of MarketResearch.com (Washington, D.C.)

For more information about market research sources, see section 6A.

2 B | LESBIAN TRAVEL: WOMEN FIRST, THEN LESBIANS

Travel experts in lesbian tourism and hospitality point to a few key concepts regarding lesbian travel. A common refrain is "As travelers, lesbians identify as women first, and as lesbians second." For lesbians, as for most women, travel safety is paramount. The presence of children in the household also affects lesbian travelers' behaviors and decisions, and in general lesbians are far less motivated by the possibility of romantic encounters than gay men are.

Merryn Johns is the editor in chief of *Curve,* the world's largest lesbian magazine. First published in 1990, the magazine now reaches 250,000 women via each print issue in the United States and an additional 150,000 women globally through digital media. Johns describes the magazine as a lifestyle magazine that mirrors lesbian life and culture with features on fashion, travel, leisure activities, and weddings.

"Out of the LGB and the T, the L needs a bit more help with its visibility," Johns says. "We are women first, then lesbians. When lesbians travel and leave home, the first thing visible about them is their gender, not their sexual orientation." She continues, "The most important thing for us when we (as lesbians) buy a product or travel overseas is safety. It is a fact that our gender will be read first because when we travel as lesbians we are not read as a lesbian first—unless you have a really masculine gender expression. You are read by another culture as a woman first. With that comes safety issues and how you are going to be treated and gender discrimination."

In addition, Johns points out, a third of *Curve*'s readers have kids. These women put their role as a parent before their sexuality.

Johns says, "Everyone needs lesbian ad creative. The days are gone now of just slapping a rainbow flag on it and trying to sell it to us. The rainbow is a powerful symbol for our community. It is a symbol that tells us that we are all welcome where we identify along the spectrum. But, for women—and you are just targeting women, and they want to be spoken to—it is really important that you represent them authentically as beings in this world." Among *Curve* magazine readers, 87 percent say that "if the company advertises to them genuinely and consistently, they will seriously consider purchasing their services."[1]

Johns advises that imagery and language are very important when it comes to targeting lesbian consumers, who have a reputation for being elusive and quite critical (see Figure 5). In addition, many lesbians are anti-consumerist and bring their political beliefs and concerns to all aspects of their lives. So if you want to advertise to the lesbian community, you have to get your message right and make sure it is authentic.

The most important guideline is simple: talk *to* lesbian consumers, not *about* them or *at* them. If you are investing in creative, get a sense of whom you are talking to because you shouldn't invest in stereotypes. Johns describes her modus operandi at

Curve: "The reality now is that we at *Curve* have to work hand in hand with advertisers. The message with the advertisers should dovetail nicely with the message of the editorial. [We've been working with] the City of Stockholm and Visit Sweden for four years now. We give them a lot of editorial support because they are genuine about targeting the lesbian consumer, and they have a very good product and the values that *Curve* shares."

INTERNATIONAL PERSPECTIVE

STOCKHOLM'S LEADING LADIES

Out Now Global, working for the Stockholm Visitors Board, developed a campaign called Stockholm's Leading Ladies (see Figure 6). This campaign focused on the lesbian market and repositioned the city with these target visitors in mind. Out Now served as the creative, media planning and buying, and public relations (PR) agency. The campaign focused on the "ideal" weekend for eight women living in Stockholm. Out Now purchased media in LGBT titles in the United Kingdom and focused on prize giveaways of trips to Stockholm for winning entrants. Out Now also relied heavily on social media through Facebook and a dedicated LGBT blog. Stockholm's Leading Ladies became Stockholm's most successful social media campaign to date.

Another advertiser that *Curve* loves working with is Key West, Florida, because Key West gets its advertising creative right. The creative executions feature beautiful images that are kind of like fantasy images—but not *too* fantasy. None of the ads features size-zero models with press-on nails. Johns explains, "That's how I want to look on vacation. That's how I want to be. The taglines are a bit of a wink and nod to the reader. It is saying, 'We understand what you want when you go on a vacation.' One of my favorite ads is the one with two women having breakfast in a beautiful Key West guesthouse. The tagline is 'Breakfast with Tiffany.' "

In what ways are lesbian travelers and gay male travelers similar and in what ways are they different? Johns points to these key differences:

1. Lesbians are more likely to travel as a couple and not seek to meet other people (in contrast to gay men, who are more likely to be looking for a sexual experience).

2. Lesbians are more likely than gay men to plan travel around romance: a honeymoon, wedding, or anniversary, or to celebrate a new relationship. Taking that first trip together can be a milestone.

3. Lesbians look for value for their money. They tend to be loyal to a destination where they previously had an enjoyable experience.

4. Lesbians are more likely to feel invested in the political climate and human rights record of the destinations they visit. If a place has a bad ecological mindset or a history of animal cruelty or minority oppression, they might be reluctant to visit. Lesbians value access to nature rather than culture, which gay men feel more attracted to.

5. Lesbians often expect trips to be transformative in some way. This desire for self-discovery, transformation, enlightenment, or romance is a common goal of women's travel. Some of the most successful travel writing of the last twenty years (*Under the Tuscan Sun; Eat, Pray, Love; Wild*) focuses on the transformative aspects of women's travel.

Johns also notes the similarities between lesbian travelers and gay male travelers:

1. Lesbians and gay men travel for LGBT events like Pride and other events that affirm their sexual identity.

2. Lesbians and gay men are more likely to support destinations and tour operators that contribute to the LGBT community in some way. Historic awareness of community and the efforts of HIV/AIDS charities have helped boost destinations like Key West and Fort Lauderdale as LGBT travel destinations.

3. Lesbians' and gay men's travel interests converge as they age and have families. Both groups appreciate and like traveling with their pets.

TOP GLOBAL LESBIAN EVENTS

Johns notes that lesbian events are a proven driver of tourism for lesbians. Table 2.1 lists popular global events drawing thousands of lesbian travelers annually.

Table 2.1 Global Lesbian Events

The Dinah	Palm Springs, California
Dinah Shore Weekend	Las Vegas, Nevada
L-Beach	Hamburg, Germany
Girlie Circuit	Barcelona, Spain
WomenFest	Key West, Florida
Aqua Girl	Miami, Florida
Provincetown for Women	Provincetown, Massachusetts
Large city Pride festivals	New York City, San Francisco, other cities

TOP DESTINATIONS FOR LESBIANS

Although the top destinations for lesbians have changed over the years with the spread of marriage equality, these are among the most popular destinations:

- New York and San Francisco are the biggest draws and perennial favorites.

- Hawaii and Key West are tops for those seeking leisure and romance.

- Orlando is popular with families because the dollar stretches further and there's plenty for kids to do.

TIPS FROM THE EXPERTS

CUSTOMIZING YOUR TRAVEL PRODUCT TO THE LESBIAN TRAVELER

Tanya Churchmuch is an accomplished public relations professional with expertise in lesbian travel. Churchmuch owns the PR agency MuchPR; served as assistant director of International Media Relations and Leisure Markets at Tourism Montreal; founded one of the first travel websites dedicated exclusively to lesbian travel; and served as chair of the International Gay and Lesbian Travel Association.

Churchmuch observes: "There are definitely more cultural differences among lesbians by their nationality. For example, German lesbians are more political and [more likely to] stay at women's inns than the French." She advises, "Get the basics before the deep details."

Do lesbian stereotypes and identities play a role in marketing to "lipstick lesbians" or butch, genderqueer, and tomboy lesbians? Churchmuch says no; rather, lesbian travelers respond better to age-related marketing than to niche marketing.

How do you ensure that your travel product and marketing are in touch with the lesbian traveler? Churchmuch advises you to ask these questions:

- Do you reach out to lesbians in your marketing?
- Are you using real lesbians or stock images in your marketing?
- Are you including lesbian images as part of mainstream outreach?
- Do you know and work with the local lesbian community?
- What amenities are available for lesbian travelers?
- How safe is your destination?
- Are your employee policies friendly to the LGBT community?
- Are you using appropriate language?

2C | BISEXUAL TRAVEL: IDENTIFYING AN ELUSIVE POPULATION

Who are the Bs in LGBT travel? We asked Zachary Moses, director of marketing and tour development for HE Travel, Key West, Florida. HE Travel is named for Hanns Ebensten, who pioneered gay travel in 1973 when he took groups of gay men rafting through the Grand Canyon and to Carnival in Rio de Janeiro.

According to Moses, "Yes, there is bisexual travel, but you won't find that name or label anywhere. Just about every tour we sell has a bisexual person on it, though you wouldn't necessarily know that. There are loads of bisexual travelers, and I would argue that they outnumber gay and lesbian travelers. A lot of gay men aren't comfortable with their own label as gay and may even love sex with women, but the gay label is easier in a lot of ways than the bisexual label, because people can understand gay, whereas many people just don't understand or even believe in bisexuality."

Moses points out that it can be difficult to reach bisexual travelers. "It's really tough to reach them since essentially they move in and out of closets. For example, as a bisexual person, when I market a gay travel company and I talk to a gay guy, the sales are better if I let him assume I'm gay. With straight people I let them assume I'm straight. When I go to gay-unfriendly places, I put on my straight hat. When I say I'm bi, there is a negative reaction among both groups. The more I talk to people, the more I realize there is a mass of people like me. Most bi people I know are in a monogamous relationship with one gender. It's not like every bi person is a swinger. In general, you can reach bi people through regular lesbian or gay marketing communications in the hope you can catch them at the time they are in a same-sex relationship."

Nonetheless, marketers can follow a few key guidelines when communicating with the bi segment of the LGBT market.

- **Remember that bisexuals live their lives having to make choices.** Don't take their choices away. Avoid saying "gay" only because this group excludes bisexuals. In fact, many bisexual people don't want to be labeled at all.

- **Avoid clichés.** Bisexuals deal with many negative stereotypes: they can't be trusted; they're all swingers; they can't commit; they're afraid to make a choice. Marketers should avoid any wording or communication that even hints at these clichés.

- **Be inclusive.** Bisexual men and gay men enjoy the company of men; bisexual women and lesbians enjoy the company of women. "Gay travel" and "lesbian travel" are exclusive, whereas bisexual by definition is open and inclusive. Convey your inclusiveness in your campaign.

For many years, the vast majority of research and marketing efforts have focused on the gay and lesbian segments of the LGBT market. That situation is changing with the efforts of Richard Gray, managing director for the LGBT Market for the Greater Fort Lauderdale Convention and Visitors Bureau. Gray is leading an important effort to understand and invite transgender travelers to Greater Fort Lauderdale (see Figure 7).

In partnership with Community Marketing & Insights (CMI), Gray launched what is called the first-ever transgender travel survey in 2014. We summarize some of the survey's key findings here. The results may surprise you.

THE TRANS TRAVELER PROFILE

Research shows that trans travelers are mostly white, highly educated, and young. In CMI's survey of seven hundred transgender travelers, the vast majority indicated that they are white or of European descent (81 percent); the next largest categories were Latino/Hispanic (9 percent), mixed (8 percent), and African American (7 percent). (The total exceeds 100 percent because multiple answers were allowed.) Fully 59 percent of respondents had a college or postgraduate degree. Just under 50 percent of the total was between the ages of thirty-five and fifty-five.

Unlike gay travelers, trans travelers are more likely to travel solo at least sometimes (62 percent). About half tend to travel with a partner or spouse. Relatively few (18 percent) indicated that they typically travel with trans friends, but over a quarter (29 percent) travel with LGBT friends. Trans travelers are more likely to define themselves as budget travelers (54 percent). Trans survey respondents also define themselves as culture travelers (48 percent) and urban core travelers (45 percent). Slightly fewer define themselves as warm-weather travelers (38 percent) and beach travelers (38 percent).

Trans respondents to the survey indicated that they take an average of two vacations per year, one business trip and one trip to visit family or friends (spending at least one night in a hotel).

TIPS TO ATTRACT TRANS TRAVELERS (FROM TRANS TRAVELERS)

In the survey completed by trans travelers for the Greater Fort Lauderdale Convention and Visitors Bureau, trans travelers offered suggestions that would help Fort Lauderdale attract trans travelers—valuable advice that should guide any destination or other marketer interested in reaching this market segment. (Numbers in parentheses indicate the percentage of survey respondents who made each recommendation.)

2C

2D

- Implement nondiscrimination and trans-friendly policies and laws to improve safety (32 percent).
- Target transgender travelers by advertising a welcoming attitude, trans-friendly businesses, and attractions in trans-specific media, LGBT media, and even mainstream media (13 percent).
- Have as many gender-neutral or single-stall bathrooms and other facilities (like changing rooms) as possible, to ensure the comfort of trans people when they are traveling (13 percent).
- Have the city provide sensitivity/transgender training not only to employees working in consumer-facing industries, including the police force and cab drivers (9 percent).
- Develop and feature trans-friendly areas and attractions, especially nightlife, in marketing communications (8 percent).
- Host trans community events, especially conventions (6 percent).
- Build and work with a strong local trans community. Appoint trans people, who can help the destination figure out how to attract and be sensitive to trans travelers, to the city tourism board (6 percent).
- Create all-inclusive ads with real trans individuals, couples, and families, rather than featuring only drag queens (5 percent).

Additional suggestions:

- Educate locals to be more trans-friendly.
- Provide trans traveler directories to show trans-friendly businesses and gender-neutral bathrooms in the area.
- Hire trans people and provide equal health-care benefits.
- Use social media to reach the trans community.
- Promote the doctors and rehab facilities in the area that understand the needs of trans travelers.
- Provide incentives or prizes for trans people to travel to a particular destination and write or share vacation stories.
- Market by word of mouth and encourage trans peer referrals.
- Use correct terminology when advertising.

WHAT'S IN A NAME?

The trans community incorporates a wide spectrum of terms that trans people use for self-definition and self-identification. It's helpful for marketers to be aware of these terms, which are listed in Table 2.2. Because the term *transgender* is used by the majority of respondents, it is the best choice for marketers trying to reach this community.

Table 2.2 Terms Used by Trans People to Describe Themselves

Transgender	54%	Gender fluid	10%
Transgender MTF	36%	Bisexual man	8%
Queer	35%	Bisexual woman	7%
Transgender FTM	33%	Heterosexual/straight man	6%
Transsexual	27%	Same-gender loving	5%
Genderqueer	27%	Intersex	4%
Pansexual	14%	Questioning	2%
Lesbian or gay woman	12%	Heterosexual/straight woman	2%
Gay man	11%		

Note: Total exceeds 100% because the survey allowed respondents to choose more than one answer.

TOP U.S. TRAVEL DESTINATIONS FOR TRANS TRAVELERS

Like their L, G, and B counterparts, trans travelers go everywhere. They tend to prefer to travel to progressive urban destinations, however. According to the results of CMI's recent survey, trans respondents visited the destinations shown in Table 2.3 on vacation and spent at least one night in a hotel.

Table 2.3 Top Ten U.S. Destinations for Trans Travelers

New York, New York	11%	Washington, D.C.	7%
San Francisco, California	10%	Philadelphia, Pennsylvania	6%
Atlanta, Georgia	10%	Los Angeles, California	5%
Las Vegas, Nevada	10%	Fort Lauderdale, Florida	5%
Chicago, Illinois	8%	Seattle, Washington	5%

Note: Numbers indicate percentage of respondents who have traveled to a given destination.

Q **Fort Lauderdale is a pioneer in LGBT tourism marketing. In 2015 Fort Lauderdale launched the world's first transgender tourism marketing campaign. How did trans travelers fit into your overall LGBT marketing program for Fort Lauderdale?**

A In 1996 Greater Fort Lauderdale launched its LGBT initiative with baby steps. We used the word *rainbow,* because *gay* seemed too risky. Over time, those baby steps have become long, powerful, purposeful, and confident strides. It was time for the Greater Fort Lauderdale CVB to emphasize the importance of the T in LGBT.

Q **Why emphasize trans travelers?**

A In LGBT tourism marketing, the T was forgotten. It is our intent to raise the bar for trans inclusion. We know a lot about lesbian and gay travelers, but little about the trans traveler. For me personally, I was motivated to develop this important and historic initiative, and equally as important, it was the right time for Greater Fort Lauderdale. Online I found the story of a truly remarkable ninety-two-year-old trans woman named Robina Asti, a former WWII pilot who transitioned to a woman and won an important legal battle regarding Social Security benefits, that inspired me and moved me to tears. I knew that tourism could become a platform in the trans movement and could make a difference. The CVB felt strongly that lesbian and gay people and our mainstream audience needed to be better informed and support-ive of trans people. I want trans travelers to Greater Fort Lauderdale to be like all travelers to Greater Fort Lauderdale: free to be themselves, free to be accepted, and, most of all, safe and welcome. We are fortunate to be in one of the most progressive counties in the state of Florida, and since 1998, Greater Fort Lauderdale has protected LGBTQ residents and visitors, barring discrimination on the basis of sexual orientation, gender identity, or gender expression in employment, housing, and lodging.

Q **How did you get started?**

A Almost two years before the launch of our campaign, I met with Commu-nity Marketing & Insights (CMI), and I explained Fort Lauderdale's intent to appeal to the trans travel market. I asked for CMI's help in assisting and developing the first-ever transgender travel survey study. It would become the largest transgender survey ever.

In early 2014 I reached out to key players in the LGBT travel space to convene a Transgender Roundtable discussion at the W Fort Lauderdale [hotel]. I called travel pioneers, including Charlie Rounds. I reached out to Masen Davis at the Transgender Law Center in San Francisco and Alexis Dee, the president of the Southern Comfort Conference, a major transgender conference that has taken place annually since 1991. The discussion also included key Fort Lauderdale community leaders, such as the president and CEO of our Pride Center and the center's director of transgender services; the executive director of SunServe and its director of transgender services; Peter Clark, the publisher of Hotspots media, the largest LGBT media group in Florida; Jeff Land from Transgender Vacations in Fort Worth, the only trans travel agency in North America; Starmark International, the CVB's advertising agency; and the maestros of CMI, Tom Roth and David Paisley.

Q What did you want to learn?

A We wanted to deeply understand travel and the trans community, including trans people's motivations for travel, as well as their preferred destinations, hotels, and travel companies and their other specific needs. We also wanted to know how Greater Fort Lauderdale can communicate respectfully with trans travelers, what training is needed here in Greater Fort Lauderdale, and how we can deliver a sensitive and authentic welcoming experience to transgender visitors.

Q Did you think that marketing to trans people would alienate other travelers?

A We wanted the millennial traveler, straight or gay, to know that we care about all of our visitors, and we wanted to inform millennials that we are a very inclusive destination with a high comfort zone. We also wanted to position the Greater Fort Lauderdale Convention and Visitors Bureau as a thoughtful and respectful leader in LGBT tourism.

Q Was this effort an image builder or a business builder?

A It is both. The Southern Comfort Conference had been in Atlanta for twenty-four years, and I was extremely excited and honored that that organization celebrated their twenty-five-year anniversary in Greater Fort Lauderdale; 525 trans people attended that conference. Jazz Jennings, a resident of Greater Fort Lauderdale who identified as transgender at four years old, was a keynote speaker. She was voted by *Time* magazine as one of the most influential LGBT youth in the world, and she is popular on all the TV chat shows, having been interviewed by Ellen DeGeneres, Katie Couric, and Oprah.

Q How did Fort Lauderdale work with the trans community to evaluate the tourism market?

A It was of the utmost importance to have the support of our local LGBT community. This had to be a team effort if it was going to be executed right and become successful. We partnered with Alexis Dee of the Southern Comfort Conference. Lexi has been by my side guiding us through this process. She is a dynamic powerhouse, an extraordinary woman, and a new friend. That said, we did need to educate LGBT travelers and residents of Greater Fort Lauderdale about the importance of embracing the trans community.

Q Tell us about the marketing campaign.

A It is our goal for Greater Fort Lauderdale to become the number-one destination of choice for trans travelers. We announced our effort on November 20, 2014, on National Transgender Day, to make our commitment more impactful and thoughtful. Our campaign uses trans images with our new message, "Where Happy Meets Go Lucky." We have added a trans landing page, www.sunny.org/TLBG, with trans travel information. Working with SunServe, we developed trans, lesbian, and gay sensitivity training for all of our hospitality partners and stakeholders. We also created a new annual Transgender Fort Lauderdale event in 2015. To our surprise, we discovered that Fort Lauderdale is home to one of the most important trans surgeons in the United States, Dr. Charles Garramone.

Emerging markets include LGBT families. Let's first define this segment. LGBT families can be any family with an openly gay family member of any age. These families are looking for inclusive family experiences that may appeal to several different generations. For example, an adult gay couple may want to take their parents on an R Family Vacation. Kids are not always a part of the equation.

LGBT families can also consist of two dads or two moms with young children or adolescents growing toward adulthood—or both. Research indicates that same-sex couples with a young child at home think "family-friendly" first, "gay-friendly" second. Demographically, LGBT parents tend to be well educated; they have dual household incomes and discretionary travel budgets.

Depending on the children's ages, the same-sex parent household will look for travel experiences that meet the family's interests at that particular stage of life—for example, a trip to Disney World for children of grammar-school age. David Ryan, who runs Rhino Africa, a mainstream tour company, and its LGBT affiliate, Out2Africa, is a gay dad who may speak for many gay dads: "With a child your reasons to travel change. Lapland became a destination on our family itinerary to see Father Christmas. You start thinking about experiences you never would have before having a kid." Lapland, located in a remote area of Finland, is the mythical home of Santa Claus. This destination can appeal to the gay male traveler's interest in discovering new places but with a keen eye on family-friendly experiences. The point here is that gay families have many options other than Disney World.

The 2016 release of *LGBT Family Travel: A Study* by the Greater Fort Lauderdale Convention and Visitors Bureau is the first major research study focusing on LGBT family travel, and it delivers a wide range of findings and insights—some that surprise and some that reaffirm conventional wisdom. The key findings are deeper and more nuanced than simply "family-friendly trumps gay-friendly":

- Most nonparent respondents indicated that they may be more likely to visit Fort Lauderdale or feel more positive about the destination because it reaches out to LGBT families.
- While they constitute only a small segment of the overall LGBT community (about 15 to 20 percent of LGBT households), LGBT families are a viable tourism segment for many destinations.

2 E

- LGBT families are less likely to travel by plane, because of both the expense and the challenges of flying with children. To attract LGBT families, air-travel outreach should focus on origin markets with the least expensive direct flights.

- Florida is the number-one state for current and future LGBT family travel, especially among those living in the South, Mid-Atlantic, Northeast, and Midwest.

- LGBT families like staying at the beach. Parents said they like the beach for three reasons: it is free, kids always have a good time at the beach, and kids can be themselves (loud and messy) and no one cares.

- LGBT parents are attracted to hotels with kid-friendly features such as water slides, which allow parents to relax and turn the kids loose. Animal-based attractions, nature walks, amusement parks, and theme parks are also important to LGBT parents.

- LGBT parents care that a destination is LGBT-friendly and has a strong local LGBT community, policies, and laws. They want to know that a destination is a safe place for themselves and their children. They largely do not care about LGBT nightlife, gay businesses, and guesthouses, however.

- LGBT parents use these three words to describe their experience with raising children: *rewarding, challenging,* and *loving.* Businesses can use these three terms or concepts to make an emotional connection with LGBT parents.

- Many LGBT parents feel quite isolated from other LGBT parents. They do not regularly interact with other LGBT parents at home, and they typically do not interact with other LGBT parents while on vacation. That said, about half desire some interaction, mostly because they perceive it to be important for their children.

- Fort Lauderdale has long been a major LGBT destination among gay men. Interestingly, gay male parents visit Fort Lauderdale more often without their children than they do with their children. Why? Statistics show that 27 percent of gay male parents have children living outside the home, and some gay men travel to Fort Lauderdale on business. This translates into an opportunity for gay men to return to Fort Lauderdale, this time with their children.

- While the general LGBT travel market can feel disproportionally gay-male-focused, gay men do not form the majority of the LGBT parents market. Lesbians and bisexual women are far more likely to be the head of a household, by a 2.5-to-1 ratio over gay and bisexual men.

- Of LGBT parents, 70 percent prefer a general vacation in an LGBT-friendly atmosphere with no specific LGBT programming; 20 percent prefer a vacation with some general LGBT programming (like a Pride event); and about 10 percent prefer LGBT family events.

- LGBT families can be especially attractive to marketers because of their preference for longer trips away. LGBT parents rarely travel with children for a quick weekend getaway, especially when traveling by plane.

Q Founded in 2003, R Family Vacations defined the LGBT family travel market. The first trip set sail in 2004 and was the subject of an HBO documentary, *All Aboard*. Why did you launch this business?

A R Family started as an LGBT family vacation company to complement what was out there, since Atlantis, RSVP, and Olivia were already established in the LGBT market. [Editor's note: See section 3G for more about Atlantis and RSVP.] We felt that it was necessary to include the family part of the LGBT travel segment. We have become a brand where you can take extended family and friends.

Q What travel products does R Family offer?

A We started by focusing on the cruise business, but we've added all-inclusive resorts and summer camps. We've also expanded to take groups on mainstream cruises.

Q R Family forged a partnership with Olivia Travel [the world's largest travel company offering chartered cruise, resort, adventure, and luxury vacations specifically to the lesbian community]. What opportunity did you see, and how did the partnership work?

A In 2016 we chartered the Hard Rock Resort in Puerto Vallarta with its capacity of up to 700 adults in double-occupancy rooms. Add in kids and we can accommodate up to 1,100. Both companies have a lot of crossover. Some of our male customers go on Atlantis, and many of our women go on Olivia. Our companies share the same philosophy about the importance of building a community on the trip and the idea that the experience is bigger than the trip. Our partnership allows Olivia to step into a new segment while maintaining the integrity of their brand, which is aimed toward travel experiences for adult women. R Family can tap into a respected forty-year-old company with a huge mailing list and one that enjoys very loyal guests.

Q How do you evaluate the product, service, or destination before you create travel products?

A It's very interesting in our segment. Most studies on the LGBT family segment show that being family-friendly is more important than being LGBT-friendly. We do both. Key West is gay-friendly but not so family-friendly. Provincetown is a great place with lots of options for kids. There are places that families already go and we wonder how to bring a gay twist to it. Summer camps exist, and we take the generic family-friendly product and make it an LGBT product. Summer camps were "takeovers." R Family programs the camp activities and books the entertainment. Everyone loves camps, but we add adult things like wine tasting and fitness classes to give the adults something to do.

Q R Family has strategic partnerships, but where else do you market?

A Facebook is a great community with many active groups. We have a big database. I miss the pre-Internet days, when I could take a quarter page as in the *Advocate* and hit the entire community. We find the most marketing success at events or by partnering with organizations where families are top-of-mind. For example, we don't market at Gay Pride events but we do go to Provincetown Family Week.

Q What are the legal implications for LGBT families when traveling?

A It can be complicated. Imagine a child going through customs and his or her parents couldn't go through together. With our first cruises, I stood on the dock and watched every family check in. Kids adopted from overseas might have had different passports from their parents. The parents knew the law, but the customs and cruise staff don't necessarily know them. Many times parents don't have the same last name as their children. In the United States, the Family Equality Council works at all levels of government to remove existing barriers by defeating legislation, policies, and practices that restrict parenting by parents who are LGBT; by promoting and passing new laws that promote LGBT parenting, such as second-parent adoption; and promoting policies and practices that are inclusive of LGBT parents.

Q What are your top tips for family-friendly LGBT marketing?

A Family comes before LGBT when dealing with LGBT families. A drag queen at a restaurant won't sell it, but kids' menus will. Be sensitive that there are young kids there. When kids with two moms are present when checking into a hotel, don't ask if the two women are sisters. Every kid with gay parents is a little ambassador for our community. "Family" desexualizes our community. By speaking to these kids who know the gay world and the straight world, they can talk about us in a mature way and they will talk to their friends.

The LGBT travel industry encompasses many aspects and businesses. Within that great diversity, we can identify the top ten modern trends in LGBT travel.

1. Businesses are rushing to the broad middle. When marketing to LGBT travelers started, it was conducted mostly in fringe cities or by small brand hotels like Starwood's W Hotels or the former independent San Francisco–based Kimpton Hotel and Restaurant Group (now part of InterContinental Hotel Group). Today LGBT outreach is conducted by major national and international brands (for example, Marriott) that cater to the wide range of tastes and budgets within the LGBT community.

2. LGBT travel is now recognized as part of the entire economic spectrum. LGBT travel was originally defined as a luxury market. Today it is recognized as a market composed of people from across the economic spectrum.

3. Interest in the LGBT family market is growing. In 2016 research regarding households with LGBT parents found that these families consist of 30 percent Gen X lesbians with children in the household compared to just 5 percent of Gen X gay men. Baby boomers do not represent a significant part of the LGBT family market. When a same-sex couple become parents, their priorities often change; they begin to seek out businesses that are LGBT-friendly or family-friendly. Given a choice, they will choose family-friendly over LGBT-friendly, but now they can do both. In terms of the future, 50 percent of millennials (both gay men and lesbians) say that they plan to have kids when they have a stable relationship. The question is: Will the market change over time, as more millennial gay men and lesbians start families? (For more information about the LGBT family market, see section 2E.)

4. The gay male market is still composed mostly of DINKS. Gay men are mostly still a "dual income, no kids" (DINK) market, though, as noted in point 3 above, more gay millennials may opt to have children in the future.

5. The all-gay guesthouse is losing ground. A few major resort towns (most notably Provincetown, Palm Springs, and Fort Lauderdale) support the remaining gay guesthouses, but integration is the trend. To survive, the all-gay guesthouses need to establish a relationship with younger gay men. (For an in-depth look at one of America's best-known gay guesthouses, the Island House Key West, see section 3K.)

6. LGBT baby boomers have money, and they're willing to spend it. Though boomers have a lot of money, there is little direct marketing to this segment. For the first time in history, there is a reachable market segment of out gay men over fifty. (The previous generation was decimated by AIDS.) This is a generation with plenty of disposable income, a propensity to travel, and a willingness to self-identify as gay. Reaching these boomers, who are looking for different travel opportunities, can be relatively easy.

7. The top travel destinations in the United States are stable. It is difficult for destinations to crack into the top-five "most visited" destinations. That said, New Orleans is coming back after the Hurricane Katrina setback. Orlando is also seeing an increase in visitors, probably because of Disney's popularity with LGBT families, events like Gay Days Orlando, and its destination-wide LGBT marketing effort.

8. More countries on more continents are reaching out to the LGBT traveler. LGBT travel is no longer just about North America. Asia, South America, Central America, and Africa are trying to attract LGBT travelers. For more information, see Chapter 5 of this handbook.

9. Advertising creative is getting more creative. At one time, advertising was all about shirtless gay men, but many marketers are moving beyond beefcake. Philadelphia, Las Vegas, and even Campbell's Soup and Oreo Cookies are using humor to get travelers' attention through smart ads on TV and in other media.

10. The "dream market" under-indexes on casino expenditures. CMI research shows that LGBT travelers underperform on gaming spending. LGBT people don't feel comfortable on the gaming floor. Las Vegas and other gaming companies, such as Caesars Entertainment and Borgata Hotel Casino & Spa in Atlantic City, however, are making significant strides.

2G | TRAINING, STAFF, BUSINESS POLICIES, AND EMPLOYEE RESOURCE GROUPS

Out Now is a global consulting company focused on understanding and meeting LGBT people's needs as customers and as employees. It specializes in workplace diversity, consumer research, and marketing. By analyzing the data gathered in the Global LGBT 2030 study (which surveyed LGBT people living in twenty-four countries on five continents), Out Now determined that the number-one factor (after price) that influences the LGBT travel purchase decision is the question "Will I feel welcomed?"

Training staff in proper business procedures and etiquette—and reaching out to other local businesses and law enforcement—is essential to making LGBT travelers feel welcome. Fortunately, companies have access to several out-of-the-box training programs that can get employees up to speed quickly.

For example, Out Now offers Gay Comfort®, an online management training workshop and certification program that helps hotels and travel agents understand the LGBT traveler. Gay Comfort covers stereotypes, phrases to use and to avoid, and up-to-date insights on same-sex weddings, honeymoons, and topical interests. It covers sensitivity not only to lesbians and gay men, but also to bisexual and trans people. Once businesses complete the Gay Comfort program, they are "Out Now Certified." Out Now Certified businesses can sell their travel product to consumers online at www.welcome.lgbt.

Members of the hospitality industry can also join the "Out Now Business Class," a professional trade association that seeks to create business opportunities and provides members with data, information about trends, and networking opportunities. Membership is free.

Another well-respected program is Community Marketing's TAG Approved program, which focuses primarily on North America. TAG (originally The Alternative Group) Approved is Community Marketing's effort to qualify businesses with certain criteria to assist LGBT travelers with purchasing travel products—such as hotel rooms—from suppliers who are authentically supporting the LGBT community.

LGBT travelers often do not wish to support companies that discriminate against LGBT people. The Human Rights Campaign's Corporate Equality Index is America's premier benchmarking tool for LGBT workplace equality (see section 1A). The data clearly demonstrate the positive economic effects of LGBT diversity policies, which increase productivity and decrease retraining and rehiring costs by retaining more LGBT staff over time. According to Out Now's research, businesses can expect average increases of 15–30 percent in productivity from employees who "feel valued as a member of my workplace team" and from workers who become "out to all." Businesses can also expect to see, on average, 5–22 percent increased retention of previously closeted workers, who had been planning to leave the company.[2]

Another business practice that leads to a high level of satisfaction among, and retention of, LGBT employees is the establishment of employee resource groups. Companies in the airline industry have been pioneers in the creation of these groups. For example, EQUAL is the United Airlines LGBT business resource group. It is a significant element of the airline's diversity and inclusion business strategy. United's EQUAL group establishes liaisons with employees, business partners, and customers. It also worked with United's procurement organization to discuss the importance of LGBT suppliers and vendors for United. The company's advertising team consulted EQUAL on the LGBT imagery used in its marketing, as well as its participation in Pride

2 G

events and in special projects like Equality Illinois's marriage planning guide (see Figure 11). EQUAL also lobbies United to advocate publicly for LGBT causes.

INTERNATIONAL PERSPECTIVE

HOMOPHOBIA IN THE WORKPLACE

Out Now's Global LGBT 2030 study, "The Power of Friends: How LGBT Allies Are Transforming Business and Society," included a specific question on homophobia in the workplace. The country with the least amount of observed homophobia in 2014 was Germany (see Figures 8 and 9), and the country with the most was Brazil, followed closely by India.

DISCUSSION QUESTIONS

1. Explain the importance of understanding and marketing to each aspect of the L, G, B, and T travel market.
2. Discuss the similarities and differences between gay travelers and lesbian travelers.
3. What are some questions that you need to ask to ensure that you are properly marketing to lesbian travelers?
4. How can your organization incorporate the tips provided in this chapter to welcome transgender travelers?
5. Table 2.3 lists the top-ten U.S. travel destinations for transgender travelers. Where does your destination rank (if anywhere)? Why? How can you help your destination land higher on the list?
6. What are some of the staff training programs developed to create a more welcoming environment for LGBT travelers?
7. What are the benefits of ranking highly on the Human Rights Campaign's Corporate Equality Index?
8. Of the top current trends in LGBT travel listed in this chapter, which are the most important to your organization? Why?

Gay men and lesbians gamble just like everyone else. According to Michael Bertetto, SLS Las Vegas (formerly with Wynn Las Vegas and Encore), however, they might be more closeted on the gaming floor or appear to be just like every other gambler: "I mean, how many times have you seen a gay guy jump up and down like he is on *The Price Is Right* at the roulette table when he wins? Likely, you will not hear 'Hey girl' at the slot machine either—even if it is a *Sex and the City* slot machine."

That said, the LGBT traveler provides many opportunities for plenty of gaming and nongaming revenue. Just as in other industries, loyalty can be built up within the LGBT community, and high-quality employees are always in demand.

Borgata Hotel Casino & Spa, Atlantic City's market-leading casino-resort, launched "Out at Borgata" in an effort to create new business as the casino industry seeks to diversify beyond its traditional reliance on gaming revenue. Borgata received a perfect score of 100 percent on the Human Rights Campaign's 2016 Corporate Equality Index (CEI) and joined the ranks of 407 major U.S. businesses that earned top marks in 2015 (see Figure 10).* The CEI rates 1,027 businesses on LGBT-related policies and practices, including nondiscrimination workplace protections, transgender-inclusive health-care benefits, competency programs, and public engagement with the LGBT community. Borgata's efforts in satisfying all the CEI's criteria resulted in its perfect score and a designation as a Best Place to Work for LGBT Equality.[†]

Tom Ballance, president and chief operating officer of Borgata Hotel Casino & Spa, says, "This recognition honors the core values of Borgata, which we have always been committed to, by supporting diversity and equal employment for all team members."

Also in 2016 Caesars Entertainment Corporation was awarded its sixth consecutive perfect rating from the CEI. One of the world's largest gaming companies, Caesars is a major supporter of the LGBT community and seeks to provide a world-class experience for all its guests. LGBT guests are treated with the utmost respect and are encouraged to take part in LGBT events and products, including gay weddings and commitment ceremonies, honeymoon packages, nightlife, and Pride events.

* For the complete Human Rights Campaign report for 2016, see http://hrc-assets.s3-website-us-east-1 .amazonaws.com//files/assets/resources/CEI-2016-FullReport.pdf.

† Ibid.

AMERICAN AIRLINES

For over two decades, American Airlines has been a pioneer in its fair-minded policies and practices for its lesbian, gay, bisexual, and transgender customers and employees. American has consistently held the highest possible ranking on the Human Rights Campaign's Corporate Equality Index, and it remains the most gay-friendly of all U.S. airlines through its partnerships with the LGBT community; loyalty and respect for customers, employees, and shareholders; and unflagging commitment to diversity. For example:

- American was the first major airline to implement same-sex domestic partner benefits (2000) with equal health-care benefits and travel privileges for same-sex partners and spouses of LGBT employees.
- American was the first major airline to include both sexual orientation (1993) and gender identity (2001) in its workplace nondiscrimination policies.
- American was the first major airline to join with 378 leading U.S. corporations to support marriage equality for same-sex couples in a friend of the court brief to the U.S. Supreme Court in the landmark case of *Obergefell v. Hodges* (2015).
- American Airlines took public stands in 2014 and 2015 in Arizona, Texas, and North Carolina to oppose discriminatory "religious freedom" legislation that would allow business owners and associates to discriminate against customers if they believe that accommodating them conflicts with their religious beliefs.
- American was the first major airline to endorse the Employment Non-Discrimination Act (2008) as well as the Tax Equity for Health Plan Beneficiaries Act (2009), which treats taxation of health insurance benefits for domestic partners the same as it does benefits for married spouses.
- American was the first major airline to have a company-recognized LGBT employee resource group—today called Pride and originally formed in 1994. Pride's mission is to work with management to embrace the principles of fairness, acceptance, and diversity in all company policies and programs.
- American was the first Fortune 100 company to pioneer an entirely gay and lesbian national marketing and sales team, the Rainbow Team. While the Rainbow Team is no longer separately identified, the airline remains dedicated to the LGBT segment through the airline's marketing, sales, and employees. American's LGBT employee resource group is a concept that many other airlines have emulated (including United and Porter).

3

BUSINESS OPPORTUNITIES

CHAPTER SUMMARY

This chapter covers the following business opportunities in the LGBT travel segment: LGBT tourism and hospitality businesses; LGBT events, festivals, and sporting events; LGBT sports to drive revenue and visitation; Pride festivals; tailoring your mainstream product with an LGBT twist; welcome signs and symbols; the cruise industry; LGBT tour operators; gays and the motor coach; airlines; hotels and lodging; meetings, conventions, and business groups; milestone celebration travel; and navigating controversies and turning them to your advantage.

KEY TERMS

LGBT tourism
Gay Pride
Black Pride
LGBT events
"bear" events
leather and fetish
gay ski week
LGBT sports
"Gayborhood"
gay cruises
LGBT tour operators
airlines' LGBT marketing
celebration travel
Religious Freedom Restoration Acts
    (RFRA)

Guaracino, Jeff, and Salvato, Ed, *Handbook of LGBT Tourism and Hospitality*
dx.doi.org/10.17312/harringtonparkpress/2017.03.hlgbtth.003
© 2017 by Jeff Guaracino and Ed Salvato

How do you create a business opportunity that taps into the global economic power of the LGBT traveler? The answer depends on your business goals, product, staff, marketing, and position in the marketplace. This chapter covers different businesses and destinations that have created new business opportunities within the LGBT travel segment.

3A | LGBT TOURISM AND HOSPITALITY BUSINESSES

It appears there are now more "out" LGBT customers than at any other time in history. As a result, you have a significant opportunity to expand your business with new customers when you combine the LGBT demographic with the boomer, Gen X, and millennial generations. Combine these people with a more globally connected economy, in which "coming out" is more accepted, where technology connects people, and where marketers can reach these customers, and you have a viable market segment. For example, as you read this, the first-ever generation of "out travelers" is celebrating marriages, honeymoons, and milestone birthdays with small- and large-group travel.

To begin, do an audit of your organization. How do you know you are gay-friendly? Conduct an honest evaluation of your product or service. Talk to your staff, colleagues, and stakeholders, including your investors, customers, management, board of directors, and political leadership. Meet with LGBT marketing experts or consulting companies (see section 6A).

COMPANY SPOTLIGHT
HILTON
In the hotel industry, it is all about "heads in beds." In March 2012 Hilton launched Stay Hilton. Go Out, the hotel's first marketing campaign targeting leisure business from lesbian, gay, bisexual, and trans travelers. Hilton also sought to improve its corporate reputation within the LGBT community. In just ten months, the Stay Hilton. Go Out package generated more than $200,000 in revenue and approximately 830 nights booked. Hilton credits tens of thousands of dollars in additional revenue from guests accessing hilton.com/GoOut and booking higher-priced accommodations.*
* Public Relations Society of America 2013 Silver Anvil Award of Excellence Winner—Multicultural Public Relations—Business, http://cite.nwmissouri.edu/ic/29-460/2013_SilverAnvils/Stay_Hilton_Go_Out_Hilton_Targets_LGBT_Travelers_w.pdf.

So let's get to the specific questions you should ask.

Question 1 **Is there a specific type of LGBT traveler who is more inclined to be your customer?** For example, if women love your product, would a lesbian like it—and if so, why? If you are you an outdoor adventure company specializing in upscale adventures to exotic locations, your LGBT customer may mirror your heterosexual customers in terms of age, household income, geographic location, and reasons for traveling. By reaching out to possible LGBT customers in a customized way, you may enhance their brand loyalty or distinguish yourself from the competition.

Question 2 **What are some of the benefits of marketing to the LGBT community?**
- An LGBT marketing effort can influence other customer segments, helping boost your business and build loyalty.
- Marketing to the LGBT community can align you with other forward-thinking, liberal, and "cool" companies and destinations. Washington, D.C., is just one destination that is positioning itself as "cool" (see Figure 12).
- Some destinations report that mainstream tourists follow the cues of LGBT travelers. Amsterdam Pride, with its flotillas of jauntily festooned and animated canal boats, was once a niche event popular with locals and some gay tourists. But it now attracts a huge percentage of the city, along with gay and straight tourists alike.
- A distinct campaign or development of an LGBT product can have a positive effect on the friends, families, and allies of LGBT people who see your company reaching out to their LGBT friends, family members, or colleagues. This benefit, however, is an important but ancillary bonus. You should not opportunistically design your LGBT product development or marketing campaign to influence your liberal heterosexual customer.

Philadelphia reported a positive response by people—gay and straight—who thought that that city's gay campaign meant that "Philly = cool." Gay stereotypes played a positive role in marketing Philly as an LGBT-friendly destination. These stereotypes can be summarized as "Gays love nightlife, appreciate arts and culture, and want to discover the next 'it' destination." Meryl Levitz, president and CEO of the Greater Philadelphia Tourism Marketing Corporation, said that the destination's groundbreaking Philadelphia Get Your History Straight and Your Nightlife Gay® "put a hipper image on the Philadelphia brand while still reaching our core market."

Question 3 **Could there be a business threat if you "come out"?** Some companies are reluctant to openly market to the LGBT community. They may disagree with marketing to the LGBT customer for political or religious reasons, or company leadership can simply be bigoted. That said, there is no evidence in the last decade that there has been an effective boycott of or negative consequences to a business that markets to the LGBT community—despite loud threats from mostly conservative activist groups, some of which use the word "family" in their name.[1] For more information, see section 3N.

LGBT events, festivals, and sporting events can enhance a destination and become reliable sources of LGBT group business. LGBT events have many benefits.

- The events can help focus a community's efforts and create and strengthen the connective tissue between the LGBT community and local and national civic (both mainstream and gay), corporate, nonprofit, and government entities.
- Over time LGBT events can become a destination-defining tourism draw. LGBT events can cultivate loyal LGBT tourists who return to the destination annually for an LGBT event or for a leisure, business, or convention purpose because they felt welcomed and had a good time.
- LGBT events can be a catalyst for social change and at times can invite controversy, debate, and opposition. In our experience—and we have found no evidence to the contrary—the controversies have led to long-lasting, positive change. In other words, the short-term negative becomes a long-term positive. No pain, no gain.

LGBT events can be large, small, or anywhere in between. Size does not matter, but quality certainly does because LGBT visitors, like all visitors, want a good experience. These events can range from small regional community Gay Pride events to large-scale national and international events. For example:

- They can be corporate-focused—for example, a meeting of a professional networking group or professional resource group.
- They can be sports-oriented: the participants take part in softball, swimming, rodeo, tennis, aquatics, and other physical activities.
- They can be large-scale fund-raisers for nonprofit organizations held in hotel ballrooms, museums, and other event spaces.

LGBT events can also be organized for affinity groups within the LGBT community, such as "bear" events. (*Urban Dictionary* defines a bear as "a term used by gay men to describe a husky, large man with a lot of body hair.") The appeal of a bear event for participants is that it tends to draw men within the gay community who not only appear much like themselves but also have similar likes, dislikes, senses of humor, and behaviors.

Another gay sub-community is composed of "circuit queens." (*Urban Dictionary* defines a circuit queen as "a gay man, usually between the ages of 30 and death, who frequents circuit parties in large cities . . . [and is] typically identical both physically and intellectually to the other . . . circuit queens in attendance.") The circuit is a series of destination parties around the world, usually themed, such as the White Party or Winter Party in Miami and Black and Blue in Montreal. Parties can last days and can draw thousands of LGBT visitors.

There is big business in events that appeal to the men in the LGBT community interested in leather and fetishes. These events are an outward expression of sexual identity through dress, sexuality, and expressions of masculinity. Numerous major cities host fetish, and especially leather-oriented, events, such as San Francisco's Folsom Street Fair, Folsom Europe, New York City's Folsom Street East, Chicago's International Mr. Leather, Washington, D.C.'s Mid-Atlantic Leather, and Amsterdam's Leather Pride. These events draw thousands of tourists who spend lots of cash.

The Mid-Atlantic Leather weekend is held each January at the Hyatt Regency Hotel in Washington, D.C. This event generates so much food and beverage revenue that in 2014 the hotel converted part of its check-in desk to a bar to accommodate the demand, and it converted the ballroom space into a dance floor with a daytime expo of leather and fetish products for sale.

> **TIP!**
>
> For events like fetish fairs, make a plan for that period that encompasses communications aimed at other guests outside that niche who may be considering booking during the event.

THE FOLSOM STREET FAIR: SAN FRANCISCO

The City and County of San Francisco's Office of Economic Analysis (OEA) conducted an economic analysis report called *The Economic Impact of San Francisco's Outdoor Events* (April 2015). The report considered (among other non-LGBT events) the economic impact of the fetish-oriented Folsom Street Fair on the city's economy. According to the report:

- The 2014 Folsom Street Fair expected 200,000 visitors, according to data provided by the event's organizers.
- Of the attendees, 29 percent were out-of-town visitors, and 71 percent were San Francisco residents.
- Among the out-of-town visitors, 89 percent stated that the Folsom Street Fair was their main reason for visiting San Francisco.
- Spending at the event, including spending by San Francisco residents, was estimated at $21.7 million.

- Estimated total visitor spending was $94.6 million. Of this spending, 14 percent occurred at the event itself, and the remaining 86 percent occurred at other local businesses not connected to the event.
- The total visitor impact of the Folsom Street Fair is estimated to be $180.8 million, including $40.5 million at retail trade establishments, $33.9 million at restaurants, and $14.5 million at hotels.
- This visitor-driven spending during the day of the event represents 283 percent of average daily retail spending in San Francisco, 349 percent of average daily restaurant spending, and 238 percent of average daily accommodations spending.

TAIPEI LGBT PRIDE

LGBT Pride in Taipei, Taiwan, has grown into the largest LGBT Pride celebration in Asia. According to Simon Tai, executive director, the 2015 event drew over 80,000 participants; close to 300,000 people flew into Taipei, some to participate in the Pride event itself, others to attend the numerous other events that have cropped up around it. Tai's volunteer-run organization pulls off this major festival with a budget of only U.S. $800,000, relying heavily on donations, fund-raising efforts, and volunteer labor. The Taiwan Tourism Bureau, the island's official tourism department, does not directly support the effort, but it does invite international LGBT media to participate and write about it. According to Tai, Taipei LGBT Pride has helped increase the visibility of the LGBT community in Taiwan.

ASPEN GAY SKI WEEK

Aspen Gay Ski Week is an annual, weeklong gay ski event in the United States. It has become a model for other gay ski weeks around the world. Worldwide gay winter events have become so successful that Aspen Gay Ski Week incorporated as the Aspen Gay and Lesbian Community Fund, a 501(c)(3) nonprofit organization, in 1996 to address the growing competition from for-profit ski weeks.

A group of local gay men and a group of gay visitors from nearby ski clubs who met every January started the event. Over the years, the all-volunteer "let's put on a show" effort became the world's first and, for many years, the only gay ski week. Parties, dancing, and skiing were the main activities, but at its roots Aspen Gay Ski Week was an event closely tied to politics and LGBT civil rights. Starting in 1979, about a decade after the Stonewall Riots, local gay men pushed for and eventually secured gay-rights protections in Aspen—a first in the state. Boulder and Denver followed.

In 1992 a new state constitutional amendment, known as Amendment 2, was adopted. It repealed all existing gay-rights legislation in the state and prevented any further gay-rights legislation from being passed at the local or state level. The response was a boycott of Colorado tourism, which hurt Aspen Gay Ski Week. Eventually, the Colorado Supreme Court ruled that Amendment 2 was unconstitutional, and the U.S. Supreme Court affirmed the decision in 1996.

What is the economic impact of Aspen Gay Ski Week? Each year it attracts at least 5,000 visitors, injects $1.5 million into the local economy, and sells 2,500 hotel room nights.[2] Table 3.1 lists popular LGBT ski weeks.

Table 3.1 Popular LGBT Ski Weeks

Aspen Gay Ski Week	Aspen, Colorado
Elevation Utah	Park City, Utah
Telluride Gay Ski Week	Telluride, Colorado
European Gay Ski Week	Various sites in France and Austria
Gay Snow Happening	Sölden, Austria
Gay Ski Week Queenstown	Queenstown, New Zealand
Whistler Winter Pride	Whistler, British Columbia, Canada

Ski events are fun and games, but they are big business, too. For example, Canada's Whistler (British Columbia) Winter Pride ski week has the following effects on the local economy (all figures are Canadian dollars):[3]

- The event generates an estimated $2.6 million in economic activity.

- The typical guest stays an average of 5.7 nights in the resort, spending an averageof nearly $300 a night on accommodations.

- The typical guest spends over $200 a day on activities, $240 on food and beverage, and $110 on shopping.

- The event supports $3.1 million in wages and salaries and an estimated sixty-nine-jobs, of which fifty-two jobs and $1.9 million in wages and salaries were in Whistler.

- The festival generates $332,000 in tax revenue.

3C | LGBT SPORTS TO DRIVE REVENUE AND VISITATION

Cities around the world from Amsterdam to Sydney to New York have hosted LGBT sporting events to drive LGBT tourism. There are hundreds of LGBT athletic competitions that draw anywhere from a few hundred to many thousands of tourists. From baseball and football to running clubs and swimming, there are more than one hundred competitive LGBT (but straight-friendly) sporting events. These can be local, regional, national, or international competitions.

Hosting LGBT sporting events in your destination is an effective marketing vehicle for reaching highly connected LGBT people who travel for their passion: their sport. These LGBT athletes are highly connected through social media and databases, two of the most cost-effective marketing channels available. Sporting events can also be predictable revenue drivers for the local economy.

EUROGAMES

Born in Europe, the EuroGames (officially called the European Gay and Lesbian Multi-Sports Championships) were conceived after the second Gay Games in San Francisco in 1986. The event combined sports, culture, and human rights activism. The Euro-Games started on a small scale in The Hague in 1992 and later took place in Spain, Belgium, Denmark, France, and Hungary. The 2016 EuroGames was held in Helsinki, Finland. The organization now has 10,000 members and connects gay and lesbian sports clubs throughout Europe.[4]

WORLD OUTGAMES

The World OutGames—held every four years—is built around three components: a human rights conference, cultural activities, and sporting events. The World Out-Games is sponsored by the Gay and Lesbian International Sport Association (GLISA), a democratically governed, international association of LGBT sports and human rights organizations that is modeled after existing multisport organizations. GLISA's members are international sporting federations, human rights organizations, continental associations representing sport teams and clubs from the world's major regions, and host cities of GLISA's World OutGames.

The first World OutGames was held in Montreal, Canada, in 2006. Over fifty venues in Montreal hosted events for the first World OutGames. Athletes competed in more than thirty sports. As noted above, however, OutGames is more than just a sporting event. Each OutGames includes a human rights conference that focuses on issues pertinent to the global LGBTQI (lesbian, gay, bisexual, transgender, queer, and intersex) community. The cultural component features LGBTQI bands and choruses as well as multiple themed dances, opening and closing ceremonies, and the Women's Village. Attendance at the event can reach 40,000 people. Montreal, Copenhagen, and Antwerp have all hosted the games; the first U.S. city to host the games will be Miami, in 2017.[5]

Q&A: MARKETING THROUGH SPORTS: WORLD OUTGAMES 2017

KEITH HART, COO, WORLD OUTGAMES 2017, MIAMI, FLORIDA

World OutGames 2017 has projected an attendance of 15,000 people, $150 million in economic impact, and a $15 million production budget. We talked with Keith Hart of the Miami World OutGames.

Q Can you describe the LGBT sports experience for us?

A Ten years ago, LGBT sports served an important need for camaraderie and socialization, like people getting together with like people. By 2015 camaraderie is probably the third-most important reason for LGBT sports, after the quality of play, and the number one is experience. Today there are more out gay qualified players and more places to meet and socialize than ten years ago. There are LGBT-straight alliances in schools, the Internet, Facebook, social media channels, and LGBT community centers for places for socialization.

Q Is the world of LGBT sports growing, shrinking, or staying the same size?

A Staying the same size or shrinking. It's due to acceptance. In some communities there is less of a need for an LGBT sports team. You can be out and play in local leagues and play football with all of your friends. As acceptance grows, I believe the numbers will shrink. Will they disappear? In team sports we see a need for master-level games (forty and above) and we see that growing a little bit. Though younger players are getting accepted and can play in local leagues, there is still a need for older amateur players who've always played on their gay teams, and that's been their camaraderie for ten years.

Q What was the bidding process for the 2017 World OutGames?

A It is a competitive bid and GLISA [Gay and Lesbian International Sports Association] holds the rights. A city or community that is interested seeks an RFP [request for proposal] from GLISA and formulates its bid committee. The first phase is a written bid that goes to the organization, outlining finance, organization, sponsors, and support from key people in government and in business. From those written proposals, GLISA narrows the list down to a small group of finalists. The next step is review by the site selection committee, and GLISA will send experts to visit your venues, meet key players, and review their checklist for a report to GLISA. At GLISA's annual bid meeting, each host city presents its plan. GLISA makes the decision.

Q From your perspective, what does it take to win the bid?

A Organization, financial wherewithal to host and produce the event, passion to be successful, and community support.

Q What tips can you share for marketing a big LGBT event internationally?

A First, you need a very creative marketing team experienced in LGBT. You want the team and leadership thinking and acting globally. Second, be consistent in your marketing. We will be marketing Miami in around forty-four countries. We have a simple five-by-seven card that covers sports, cultures, human rights, dates, and place. It is available in German, Spanish, English, Portuguese, French, Arabic, and Russian. We send it to marketing ambassadors around the world to help promote the event. Third, develop effective partnerships. For example, Miami will partner with the European Gay and Lesbian Sports Federation and several cities in a program called Out City, which is similar to the sister city program.

GAY GAMES

The granddaddy of the LGBT sporting leagues is the Federation of Gay Games, Inc., started in the United States in 1982. Like most LGBT sporting associations, the federation is primarily an all-volunteer organization. It was the first organization to create the idea of an Olympic-style sporting competition specifically for LGBT athletes. Its purpose is to foster and augment the self-respect of gay men and women throughout the world and to engender respect and understanding from the nongay world, primarily through the Gay Games, an organized, international athletic and cultural event held every four years.

The Gay Games have continually switched venues and have attracted a large number of athletes and spectators. For example, the 2014 Gay Games was held in northeastern Ohio. The competition consisted of one week of competition-based athletic events for participants of all sexual orientations, races, genders, and ages. Events included badminton, basketball, bowling, golf, racquetball, softball, swimming, and tennis, as well as many other individual and team sports.[6]

Perhaps the best economic study conducted on the effects of LGBT sporting competitions is the 2014 *Gay Games Economic Impact Study* by Shawn M. Rohlin and Nadia Greenhalgh-Stanley of Kent State University. That report indicated that the games attracted roughly 20,000 people. Approximately 75 percent of those who participated or attended the games were nonlocals. The games generated approximately $38.8 million of direct economic impact on the local northeastern Ohio economy, including higher revenues generated for local businesses and the creation of new local jobs.

> **TIP!**
>
> If you would like to explore LGBT sports as a business opportunity, consider working with a local LGBT sports organization (typically found online or in your local LGBT newspaper). One possible resource is Cyd Zeigler, a well-regarded expert on LGBT sports. He is cofounder of Outsports.com and coauthor of *The Outsports Revolution: Truth & Myth in the World of Gay Sports*.

3D | PRIDE FESTIVALS

Pride festivals are excellent opportunities to connect with the LGBT community. Marketers can align with Pride festivals in two key ways: as a sponsor or as an exhibitor. Festivals can be efficient ways to reach target customers directly. As a very cost-efficient way to connect with multicultural LGBT people, consider identifying Pride events for specific groups such as the black or Latino LGBT communities.

A possible concern is the marketing "noise" during Pride season, when many companies attempt to cut through the clutter to reach the LGBT segment. Is a Pride event the right platform on which to get your message out? The answer depends on your goals. It may also depend on where you are. If you're a big employer in a community, your absence may be considered a slight to the local LGBT community.

INTERPRIDE AND WORLDPRIDE

InterPride is the international organization that ties Gay Pride together globally. Its member organizations produce Pride events. Pride events can include a parade, march, rally, festival, arts festival, cultural activity, event, or activity organized for people identifying as lesbian, gay, bisexual, transgender, intersex, and other emerging sexual identities. InterPride produces WorldPride, a global event that raises awareness of lesbian, gay, bisexual, and transgender issues on an international level through parades, festivals, and other cultural activities. It started in Rome in 2000, then moved to Jerusalem (2006), London (2012), Toronto (2014), and Madrid (2017).[7] This event comes with global publicity, international visitors, and (in almost all host cities) controversy.

THE CENTER FOR BLACK EQUITY

The Center for Black Equity, Inc., formerly the International Federation of Black Pride (IFBP), was founded in 1999 when a coalition of Black Pride organizers in the United States, Canada, United Kingdom, and South Africa formed to promote a multinational network of LGBT Pride and community-based organizations. There are over thirty Black Pride events attracting more than 450,000 attendees each year. The Center for Black Equity is the only black LGBT international organization in the world.[8]

3E | TAILORING YOUR MAINSTREAM PRODUCT WITH AN LGBT TWIST

Larger destinations may have iconic gay neighborhoods. Examples include Greenwich Village in New York City (site of the Stonewall Riots), San Francisco's Castro, Philadelphia's "Gayborhood," and Montreal's Gay Village. Other destinations, including Manchester, England, and Tel Aviv, Israel (see Figure 13), have highly attended LGBT Pride festivals, whereas other vacation hot spots such as Provincetown (Massachusetts), Key West (Florida), and Mykonos (Greece) offer a relaxing vacation punctuated with defining special events.

Your product or destination may be extraordinary in its own right and have no obvious LGBT assets. For example, your destination may include attractions that are popular with everyone: Big Ben, the Eiffel Tower, the White House, the Statue of Liberty, or the Great Pyramids. Smart marketers have introduced a gay twist to an otherwise mainstream product to attract LGBT travel consumers. Following are three examples that leverage mainstream popular attractions by finding hidden-in-plain-sight LGBT angles. It must be noted that these marketing campaigns work because they are authentic and appropriate, and they truly enhance LGBT visitors' experiences.

1. **Oscar Wilde Tours.** Oscar Wilde Tours offers literary-themed tours of New York, London, Paris, Greece, and Italy. In each destination the company explores the often hidden and purposely expunged history of same-sex love. In New York the tours cover neighborhoods important in the gay civil rights movement. The company also features a gay tour of the Metropolitan Museum of Art, an example of how an innovative company can take an existing product, give it a genuinely gay twist, and package it as an intriguing gay product. Professor Andrew Lear, Oscar Wilde Tours' owner and founder, leads groups on an exploration of homoerotic

art in the Metropolitan Museum. The tour encompasses art across history, from ancient Greek nudes and erotic vase painting to homoerotic paintings from the Renaissance, to modern works by LGBT artists portraying LGBT people and expressing same-sex desire. Once you really see what those men are doing standing one behind the other in otherwise easy-to-miss carved New Guinea totems representing a same-sex initiation rite into adulthood, you'll never look at them the same way again![9]

2. **The New York Botanical Garden.** The New York Botanical Garden (NYBG) hosts a series of LGBT nights with programming for people sharing the same or similar interests. The NYBG forged a partnership with the National Gay and Lesbian Chamber of Commerce in New York City. The NYBG markets the LGBT @ NYBG initiative with events throughout the year to celebrate the LGBT community and its allies. It promotes the evenings "as an opportunity to mingle with friends, colleagues, and families, or chatting with someone new."[10]

3. **Quiiky Gay Tour of the Vatican Museums.** Quiiky is the first Italian tour operator specializing in gay and lesbian tourism, an amazing achievement considering the country's conservative nature. Quiiky offers art and history tours, tasting tours, boat tours, fashion tours, and walking tours. Hundreds of Quiiky guides and tour operators offer tours of the Vatican's museums. Each tour is led by a gay or gay-friendly tour guide who leads LGBT people and their friends, families, and allies on a tour through the Vatican museums, pointing out hidden-in-plain-sight homoerotic art as well as art by famous gay artists such as Michelangelo. The unauthorized tours have generated international media coverage, including a piece in the *New York Times*.[11] A highlight of the tour is the many homoerotic images contained in the glorious art adorning the ceiling of the Sistine Chapel, from same-sex "damned souls" kissing one another to a highly erotic figure of Christ, details not discussed in the official tour books. According to Alessio Virgili of Quiiky, "This gay tour puts into context the importance homosexuality had in the Renaissance period and in Italian art itself, a role that has been hidden until now because of societal homophobia."[12]

Tours like Oscar Wilde and Quiiky are brilliant strokes of marketing and product development because they highlight the contributions of LGBT artists, inventors, explorers, entrepreneurs, writers, politicians, and others who have been suppressed, ignored, or erased. By highlighting the achievements of gay artists, marketers not only create an interesting new product with a gay twist, but they also help LGBT travelers understand and connect with the contributions of people like themselves from the past. These tours provide an enticing tidbit of the rich LGBT history that is largely hidden in the West's heteronormative culture.

3 E

3F | WELCOME SIGNS AND SYMBOLS

You can tailor your product to LGBT travelers without changing the major operations of your business. Consider these ideas and examples, which make use of widely understood welcome signs and symbols:

- If you run a visitor center, work at an information desk, or are a concierge, consider adding a rainbow pin to your jacket lapel, just as you would add a German flag for a concierge who speaks German or a French flag for one who speaks French. A rainbow pin doesn't mean the person is necessarily LGBT, just as the German flag does not indicate that the person is German. Rather, both are proficient in a specific "language."

- If you run a tour company, offer a tour led by someone knowledgeable about local LGBT history or community. Doing so doesn't change the tour, but it can make your customers comfortable asking questions they might not otherwise ask. Alternatively, develop a local LGBT history tour virtually (on your website), a live tour with a tour guide, or a self-guided tour.

- On windows, doors, or in other prominent places, display symbols such as the rainbow flag and other logos that are commonly understood by LGBT travelers, such as the Human Rights Campaign's equal sign.

- Go the extra mile. Some cruise ships host LGBT gatherings (such as a "Friends of Dorothy" meetings) to connect LGBT guests. Others go a step further and curate LGBT experiences on the ship with onboard events such as wine tastings or small group excursions in ports of call.

- Promote staff and management diversity, and make your staff visible to your customers. Diversity today includes not only LGBT staffers, but also those of varying races, ethnicities, and nationalities.

COMPANY SPOTLIGHT

THE FIRST FLOOR AND SECOND FLOOR, ROME

Hotels are plentiful near Rome's Colosseum. The First Floor and Second Floor is the first boutique hotel in the heart of Rome and in the heart of Gay Street. The property caters to international LGBT visitors. To help its guests get around Rome, the hotel created the Coming Out Roma Tour, which is available for download to a smartphone. The hotel also offers gay-friendly massage therapists and operates a coffee shop, restaurant, bar, and dance club popular with LGBT locals and tourists.

In 2015 *ManAboutWorld* magazine rated the gay friendliness and LGBT marketing efforts of mainstream cruise companies and found that cruise companies are lagging behind other hospitality industries: "The cruise industry hasn't always had a great relationship with gay cruisers. When Kevin Mossier first started chartering ships at RSVP over 30 years ago, most lines wouldn't even allow a gay group. Today, most lines are actively welcoming, if not marketing directly to LGBT customers. But when it comes to policies that actively engage LGBT customers and protect LGBT employees and guests, the lines in general are not as far along as you'd think, and in general, reluctant to discuss it."[13]

For many years, most major cruise lines simply marketed to the mainstream consumer and let gay or lesbian charter companies market their own sailings. This squandered business opportunity has been changing in recent years; a handful of companies actively court the LGBT segment, and more forward-looking brands are quite eager to appeal to gay travelers (see Figure 14).

One of the most progressive of the mainstream cruise companies is the Holland America Line, which meets every one of *ManAboutWorld*'s criteria as an LGBT-friendly cruise company. Holland America's answers to *ManAboutWorld*'s survey illustrate the steps a cruise company can take to create a safer and more welcoming experience for LGBT guests.

1. Do you promote LGBT social events on non-charter sailings?

Holland America: Yes, we offer LGBT get-togethers on every cruise. The events are introduced by a cruise staff member at the first gathering and then open to guests to host at following events. The get-togethers are always listed in the ship's daily program.

2. Do you do any marketing or outreach to the LGBT community?

HA: We market to all demographics and communities. Some specifically targeted outreach takes place with various partnerships, but our general advertising and marketing addresses our brand experience, which appeals to many groups and demographics. We also support the LGBT community through sponsorships with various organizations and support and advocacy groups. A few recent examples include the Human Rights Campaign Dinner, Taste of Greater Seattle Business Association, the LGBT Community Center in San Diego, the Seattle Men's Chorus/Seattle Women's Chorus and the National LGBTQ Task

Force in Miami. We also have had a corporate sponsorship with the Seattle Pride Parade, with employees taking part in the event for the past few years.

3. Do you do any diversity/inclusion training for employees that specifically covers LGBT?

HA: It has been, and will continue to be, the policy of Holland America to afford equal opportunity for employment to all individuals regardless of race, creed, color, religion, national origin, sex, age, marital status, sexual orientation, gender identity, veteran status, or mental, sensory, or physical disability. Therefore, all personnel matters such as recruiting, hiring, training, termination, compensation, benefits, layoffs, transfers, education, tuition assistance and social and recreational programs will continue to be administered in accordance with company policy. Diversity and inclusion [are] a part of yearly required training, online continuing education, and new employee training.

4. Are LGBT employees covered by a nondiscrimination policy?

HA: Yes, and as well in the context of state and federal employment laws. It is the company's intent to provide a work environment free from all types of discrimination. All employees are expected to be sensitive to and respectful of their co-workers and others with whom they come into contact while representing the company. We prohibit all forms of discrimination whether due to race, creed, color, religion, national origin, age, sex, sexual orientation, marital status, gender identity, disability, veteran status, or political ideology.

5. Do you provide any guidance for guests or employees when docking in countries where LGBT is criminalized?

HA: Depending on the area and concerns, we provide a ship-wide letter advising all guests if there are major concerns. The letter is general and provides an overview of the issues for the area, and invites guests to contact the front desk with concerns. It is not a standard practice with every port though.[14]

TIP!

Cruise directors should become aware of what is of interest to LGBT passengers in each port of call, in addition to the mainstream offerings. Connect with the local LGBT community. Cruise directors and entertainers should also be mindful of not making homophobic jokes or booking entertainment that might cross the line. What used to be acceptable in entertainment or as a joke is quickly losing steam as the community is increasingly mobilized against discrimination in all forms.

ATLANTIS EVENTS AND RSVP VACATIONS:
THE GLOBAL LEADER IN GAY TRAVEL

Atlantis is the most successful LGBT tour operator in the world. In 1991 its founder, Rich Campbell, started with the simple idea of a gay week on the beach with friends. Since then his company has become one of the largest buyers of travel products and has generated at least a billion dollars in revenue, all from LGBT travel. Each year Atlantis customers spend up to $100 million, making a huge impact on destinations, accommodations, airlines, and the cruise industry. Atlantis and its subsidiary, RSVP Vacations, have carried nearly 300,000 passengers, averaging 20,000 people per year. The customer base is loyal: 70 percent come back for another trip.

Atlantis Events charters more cruises than any other company in the world. For some cruise companies, LGBT charters from Atlantis can generate more revenue than all other charter business (straight or gay). Atlantis Events is among the elite tour operators that can buy and sell out megaships that hold five thousand passengers.

Campbell says that Atlantis sells a social experience. He takes a travel product—a cruise ship or a resort—and turns it into a highly valued gay product for a week to weeks at a time. "We create a social experience that is distinctive and unique in the gay community—not a singular experience but rather a series of unique experiences that our guests don't have a parallel to in their regular life of a typical passenger. That's the definition of a vacation at its most basic, breaking your routine. Our trips create a new social paradigm to enjoy; to make new friends; and for guests get to know themselves better."

Atlantis is global: 60 percent of its customer base is North American, and 40 percent of its clients come from outside the United States and Canada. Global growth has been based on word of mouth. The United Kingdom, Germany, France, Italy, and Spain are Atlantis's top international markets. Australia and Brazil are growing markets for Atlantis; so is Asia (see section 5E).

Atlantis has taken 12,000 people to Russia. According to Campbell, "Not a single passenger had anything but a warm welcome. The Russian people are nice, and the Russian gay people are super welcoming. Russia has a terrible law that allows people to abuse gay people. It makes it hard to sell a cruise experience there now." Atlantis has also set its sights on another communist country, Cuba. For Campbell, the issue is reasonable access. "The people-to-people visa places restrictions on us," Campbell explains. "If you have to spend 80 percent of your time that is educational and cultural, it diminishes Cuba as a vacation destination. I'm willing to just wait."

> Atlantis has taught the cruise lines a lot about programming their own ships. Every single cruise line has tried to emulate (not always successfully) Atlantis and apply its approach to the straight cruises—from poolside events to how the cruise director relates to the audience. Mainstream cruise lines see the social interactions on the gay cruises and want to instill that in their guests. Of course, they have their eyes firmly on the revenue side of that experience.

3H | LGBT TOUR OPERATORS

Gay tours have come a long way in a short time. Brand G Vacations, founded in 2011, promised to be "the next generation in gay travel." Brand G takes the LGBT community around the world to exotic and close-by destinations. How does the company position and market itself? Brand G sees its position in the LGBT travel space as:

1. Primarily for gays and lesbians but clearly welcoming to their friends and families
2. Priced competitively—trying to avoid the "gay premium"
3. Designing innovative trips that combine the interests of the gay traveler with the destination's offerings
4. Using the power of travel to make the world a better place.

Today there are many LGBT tour operators. Other successful LGBT tour operators include Out Adventures and Out2Africa.

OPPORTUNITIES TO WORK WITH LGBT TOUR OPERATORS

Hospitality businesses have several opportunities to work with LGBT tour operators. For example, a few mainstream tour operators have had success launching LGBT group departures. Other mainstream tour operators can tailor their products to be more welcoming to LGBT travelers. For an example, see the discussion of Kenes Tours in section 5I.

Another opportunity is for destinations, hotels, and other travel suppliers to work with LGBT tour companies to broaden their business by expanding their reach to the LGBT market. For example, Atlantis is the largest charterer of cruises (straight or gay) in the world, and it accounts for a majority of revenue generated by all ship charters for a particular company. Atlantis and other cruise and tour operators are looking for travel suppliers who not only provide top-quality accommodations and services but also understand the particular sensitivities and needs and interests of the LGBT traveler.

Robert Sharp, cofounder of Out Adventures, which specializes in scheduled group tours and tailor-made packages primarily for gay men, describes what he looks for when buying a travel product: a gay-welcoming environment. According to Sharp, "We are selling a comfortable, fun environment to explore a destination. It is very important, and our first point of discussion is whether a supplier or product is gay welcoming, that they understand the special needs and behaviors of gay travelers."

David Ryan, owner of Rhino Africa and its LGBT-specific subsidiary, Out2Africa, leads groups of LGBT travelers to several African countries that have a reputation for being unfriendly to LGBT people. Safety is one of the major concerns for first-time customers. How does Ryan evaluate "gay friendliness"? It all centers on safety and security. Ryan notes that all the top LGBT destinations have "made a point of positioning themselves as safe and secure for gay travelers." He looks at a product as a gay man himself and asks the following questions:

- Am I safe as an LGBT traveler?

- Are my rights protected as an LGBT traveler?

- How welcoming is the destination to LGBT travelers?

Sharp also values partnerships. Out Adventures collaborated with the Tourism Authority of Thailand on a 2014 LGBT project that included a media and travel agency familiarization tour and other activities.

Mainstream tour operators wishing to attract the LGBT segment can partner with a destination marketing organization. For example, Catherine Reilly, managing director of Brendan Vacations, a member of the family-owned Travel Corporation, describes her company's relationship with Discover Ireland, the destination marketing organization for the Republic of Ireland: "Normally we try to get help from Discover Ireland, which is really committed to the LGBT market. We leave it to Discover Ireland to generate interest in the destination and to make Ireland appealing to all travelers, including now of course LGBT travelers. We want them to make sure that whatever they are doing, they bring all travelers to Ireland, including LGBT travelers. The tourism board sells the destination. And Brendan comes to the market with a product. We could do advertising of specific products to this market. We'd do this with partners like Discover Ireland or Aer Lingus."

3 H

The motor coach industry in the United States and Canada consists of over 3,950 companies that operate almost 40,000 motor coaches (or, as they are called in common parlance, buses). Most (94 percent) of these companies are small and operate fewer than twenty-five motor coaches.[15] The business opportunity remains relatively slim compared to the overall industry but can be lucrative for smart small business operators.

Though charter bus companies have been less active in the LGBT segment, some companies have worked with gay tour operators and cruise charter companies such as Atlantis Events and RSVP Vacations. When a ship docks in port and the LGBT tour operator is looking for a transportation company, an opportunity is created. If you run a bus fleet, are you ready to take advantage of the opportunity?

Some bus companies have created their own niche by serving locations frequented by gay travelers and appealing to the urban LGBT communities without cars. For example, Washington, D.C.–based BestBus, headed by CEO Richard Green and his business and life partner, Asi Ohana, has a substantial gay customer base, taking passengers from the Dupont Circle area in Washington, D.C., to New York City's Times Square and to Rehoboth Beach, Delaware, in the summer months. The company sells primarily on quality, on-time performance, reliable WiFi, and bottled water for each passenger. BestBus advertises in some local gay media and supports several gay-related causes, which this segment values (and rewards).

Al Ferguson and Chuck Scott own AlandChuck.travel, one of America's largest travel companies; they run eleven offices. They specialize in cruises and tours and once a year run the "Gay Party Bus" from Orlando to Tampa's Pride festival. For prices starting at $19, passengers get round-trip transportation and slew of other benefits that help connect the two cities.

Charlie Rounds led the first gay group tours to Ireland in 2002 with Brendan Vacations. There is limited train service in Ireland, so the company offered four charter tours by motor coach. According to Rounds, the key to getting gays onto charter buses was smart programming: "It wasn't a five-hour motor coach trip. It was two 2.5-hour journeys with a cooking class at the home of a gay chef in between, all narrated by a drag queen." In this case, the trip became part of a fun, memorable, and gay experience.

A charter bus operator doesn't have to offer an all-gay program to court the LGBT market. It can simply ensure that its product or service welcomes all travelers, including those who are LGBT. If the company is pursuing the LGBT market for group tours or special-occasion charters, it should consider marketing in local gay media, being present at gay events, and contributing to local gay causes to show LGBT customers its support for the community.

Industry associations like the American Bus Association (ABA) are making inroads by including LGBT travel as part of their annual conference agendas.

3J | AIRLINES: PUTTING MORE BUTTS IN SEATS

Airlines seek competitive advantages because what most airlines sell is simply "butts in seats." Loyalty programs, prices, routes, and in-flight services such as first-class amenities are traditional ways to win new and retain existing customers. For some airlines, LGBT travelers have been an important part of a strategy to increase market share and revenues; in other words, their goal is to get additional *gay* butts in seats.

Airline LGBT marketing started in 1994 with American Airlines, which was attempting to recover from an embarrassing onboard homophobic incident. A crisis became an opportunity, which ultimately allowed American not only to survive the crisis but also to thrive in a new category that it helped pioneer: dedicated LGBT marketing. LGBT marketing continues with airlines of all sizes.

TIP!

Almost every day, airlines open a new route. No event could be more generic, even dull. To get attention, consider a smart, strategic media bonanza PR stunt to sell your seats. Air New Zealand hired the gay icon and Emmy award–winner Kathy Griffin as the official "Hostess" for the airline's first North American "Pink Flight" from San Francisco to the 2008 Sydney Gay and Lesbian Mardi Gras. The plane was wrapped in a pink feather boa. This stunt generated international media attention, but it also spoke to the important stakeholders and potential leisure and business customers in San Francisco.*

* Press release, Air New Zealand, January 2008.

MIDSIZE CARRIER: ALASKA AIRLINES

Alaska Airlines, based in Seattle and the seventh-largest airline in the United States, once was known for distributing Christian prayer cards on its meal trays (a practice discontinued in 2012 after thirty years).[16] The airline turned to LGBT tourism to stand out in a competitive marketplace (see Figure 15).

Alaska Airlines' 2015 LGBT marketing campaign illustrates a smart and successful approach to reaching the segment. Alaska started with market research that helped determine the market potential. Here is a description of the campaign and its success from Clint Ostler, manager of media and market strategy for Alaska Airlines:

For Alaska Airlines, most LGBT travelers are between twenty-five and forty-five years old, make more than $100,000 a year, are college educated, travel three to four times a year, and are active, health-conscious entertainment seekers. 6.2 percent of all travelers from San Francisco are LGBT, 4.8 percent from Seattle, and 4.6 percent from Los Angeles.

Alaska Airlines focused marketing efforts on outbound flights from Seattle, Los Angeles, and San Diego to destinations with LGBT events in the following markets: Palm Springs, Hawaii, and Puerto Vallarta. Alaska Airlines launched a new LGBT section on the airline's website, forged editorial partnerships, secured LGBT event sponsorships, developed social media engagement, and started community conversations.

Web advertising copy spoke directly to the LGBT traveler with marketing messages such as: "Who you fall in love with is not your choice. How you fly with them is. #Flywithpride."

Passengers booking on this website were able to get a 10 percent discount. The reason to book: "The LGBT community has come so far. Let us fly you the rest of the way."

Other creative advertised a $199 one-way air fare to Puerto Vallarta using this tagline: "We'd like to be your domestic partner. International, too."

We are very proud of our success: within eight months of introducing a new gay travel web page on Alaska Airlines, website traffic increased 2,096 percent. Advertising "equality for every seat" and the "pride discount" sold seats.[17]

LEGACY CARRIER: AMERICAN AIRLINES

The definitive gay-friendly American Airlines is the world's largest airline and a pioneer in marketing to the LGBT segment. It continues to set the benchmark in the airline industry for its progressive approach toward LGBT travelers and employees. For more details about American's business practices, see the Company Spotlight sidebar in section 2G.

REGIONAL INTERNATIONAL CARRIER: PORTER AIRLINES

Porter Airlines, a newcomer to the regional and international airline routes at Canada's two biggest destination cities, Toronto and Montreal, found a perfect match to their desired customer in the LGBT traveler. Compared to the legacy carrier Air Canada, Porter Airlines seems to break all the stodgy old rules. Porter flies ultra-efficient propeller planes, and the flight attendants wear classic airline uniforms, complete with pillbox hats for females. Everyone is welcome to enjoy the airline lounge—offering complimentary snacks, beverages, and espresso drinks—and Porter's advertisements take a very different approach from their competition's (Figure 16). Porter's core customers are savvy urban travelers who are looking for the quickest transportation from one point to another.

Brad Cicero, the director of communications and public affairs at Porter Airlines, says, "Porter has a diverse and inclusive culture and is proud to have many LGBT team members at all levels of the organization." Cicero summarizes Porter's outreach to the LGBT market in 2015 and 2016, which focused on building visibility among LGBT travelers by sponsoring various charity and community events: "This includes the INSPIRE Awards, an annual event recognizing top influencers and active community members. Porter team members also joined the AIDS Committee of Toronto to support the Scotiabank AIDS Walk for Life."

3K | HOTELS AND LODGING

Hotels and lodging account for a substantial portion of the LGBT travel dollar. How can hotels—from small guesthouses to mega-hotels with properties all over the world—appeal to LGBT travelers as more properties compete for the hearts and minds of this market segment? Let's look at some successful examples.

KEY WEST, FLORIDA:
SMALL ACCOMMODATIONS MARKETING PERFECTED

Key West, Florida, markets to LGBT travelers globally. Key West is a tiny island surrounded by lapis-colored water where "One Human Family" is the official motto. Key West promotes its natural beauty and eclectic charm and positions itself as a safe, seductive sanctuary where you can be out and welcomed. Key West's marketing efforts began with no budget and were limited to a few lifestyle expos and a couple of Pride events. Today Key West tells its story with creative images of locals and cutting-edge taglines in print and Internet advertising; the island aired one of the first gay television commercials—"Out Before It Was In"—on mainstream stations. Marketing now centers on LGBT press research trips, Pride event promotions, international travel trade shows, including ITB, and sponsorships and partnerships.

We talked with Jon Allen, owner of Key West's Island House, a clothing-optional, all-male gay guesthouse. It is a destination in and of itself and arguably one of the most successful gay guesthouses in history. According to Allen, the biggest change in LGBT travel over the decades is the mainstreaming of gays in United States. "As gays are more accepted, there is less need for gays to look for 'separate but equal' experiences. The number of gay guesthouses and bars is shrinking. It's still true now, as it was then, that Island House and the gay guesthouse represent a safe environment to be you."

Allen continues, "The second change is that if you have an individual business like a gay guesthouse, you need to think clearly about what you're selling. When you're selling gay travel, you're selling an experience. The Island House is selling experiences for gay men. We have more in common with Disney than with Marriott. Gay men are sophisticated; they will pay a premium for experiences they like. Do a great job, and travelers will seek your product out. With TripAdvisor and Yelp, consumers are in control of your reputation."

Third, Allen says, gay travel is changing as the mainstream hospitality and tourism companies compete for the gay dollar. "In the past, there were so few places where gay guesthouses could exist. So they are concentrated in Provincetown, Key West, and a handful of other places. A lot of them were holes in the wall and not up to the standards of the experience that a good hotel should provide. As it became more OK to be openly gay, and gays can stay at mainstream hotels and not get bothered, they chose not to stay at substandard guesthouses."

Still, Allen thinks, gay travel hasn't changed in some fundamental ways: "Gay guys want to hook up—that hasn't changed. But meeting new people has migrated online and there are more people chatting on gay hookup apps and identifying as gay on Facebook. The need to connect with other gay people exclusively in gay bars is shrinking."

Allen points to Key West's annual $1 million investment in marketing to LGBT travelers as a key to the destination's ongoing popularity. "It is a global campaign," Allen explains. "Key West has a full-time person devoted to this market, Steve Smith, sales manager for the LGBT market and self-described 'brochure fairy.' Key West is represented at twenty to twenty-five annual trade and consumer shows globally. Marketing includes national cable television and radio, plus print ads and e-mail marketing. Our marketing challenge is not to explain Key West. People understand the experience and to come as you are. Our challenge is to get people to come *now*. Liberal heterosexuals love the LGBT imagery in our mainstream advertising. Conservatives who don't like same-sex marriage are probably not interested in Key West."

SELLING "GAY" IN THE BOARDROOM: MARRIOTT SHOWS HOW #LOVETRAVELS

Marriott Hotels launched an LGBT marketing effort in 2007 that began modestly but grew into one of the most successful campaigns of all time. How did this company—not particularly well known for its outreach to the LGBT community—become a global leader in the segment? Marriott's experience shows the importance of having an indefatigable internal champion, centralized resources, external expertise, and a supportive board. This is a story of a hotel chain expanding from a $50,000 LGBT website to $5 million in funding for a diversity campaign approved at the highest corporate level and how that niche campaign drove the company's overall marketing efforts.[18]

Marriott started its LGBT marketing efforts as part of the area of responsibility that included "multicultural marketing." When Randy Griffin looked more closely at the potential market, he identified four key segments that seemed to be potentially lucrative: LGBT, African American, Latino, and Asian. None of Marriott's competitors was strong in marketing to these groups. Griffin had to supply materials to three hundred salespeople, so he brought in experts and wrote sales training guides. In the process, Griffin realized that he had the least amount of information for the LGBT segment.

Griffin's goal was to move Marriott to the forefront of LGBT outreach, but he had no approved budget. He went to the Marketing Department and got a quote for building a website: $50,000. In Griffin's words, he went "begging for funds from department to department," including Marriott Rewards and corporate communications. In the end, he got a little money from everyone; all the internal stakeholders perceived value in the LGBT market. The LGBT website was launched in six countries and in five languages.

Moving from conceptualization of this project to implementation took one year. That may seem fast, but at Marriott all the experts are in one place, which helps streamline and speed up decision making. Marriott set up a guiding committee to oversee the effort. Each area of operation went through its senior vice president for approval and also through the Global Sales and Marketing senior vice president for final approval.

By the time the website had been up and running for year, it had produced only lackluster results. Marriott had created a great website but had allocated no money to drive traffic to it. (That year also coincided with a steep economic downturn in the United States.)

In response, Marriott formed a think tank with a representative from each revenue department to brainstorm ways of driving additional revenue through the multicultural space. The vice president of marketing got $30,000 in funding to do in-depth marketing research to determine which multicultural markets represented the greatest growth opportunity. The results of the research were clear: the three biggest opportunities lay in the African American, Latino, and LGBT markets. Once the research was complete, the members of the think tank built a business case to move Marriott from third or fourth place to the number-one slot in each of these three market segments. The think tank had to present the business case to Arne Sorenson, president and chief executive officer of Marriott International, and his entire executive leadership team. It was a comprehensive business plan targeting three segments on the marketing, customer engagement, and PR/diversity fronts. Everyone in the room showed strong support for the idea. The think tank went in asking for $3 million but received more: the executive team agreed to fund the initiative at $5 million, which was needed to activate the plan across the three segments.

After receiving the approval and the budget, the team used the research to develop a brand identity for each segment and a plan to reach these travelers. Before they could implement this plan, however, the team had to conduct an honest self-audit. Marriott's reputation in the consumer market was that "It's a Mormon company that is intolerant"—a reputation it did not deserve. Marriott is in fact a publicly traded company answerable to its shareholders. There is a long list of LGBT issues that Marriott supported. For example, Marriott was the first hotel chain to offer benefits and health insurance to same-sex partners; it openly supported the Employment Non-Discrimination Act (ENDA); and it offers diversity training. Taking this support as a baseline, Marriott aligned itself with a half dozen influential LGBT groups that were not confrontational or severely activist, including the Human Rights Campaign (HRC), Parents and Friends of Lesbians and Gays (PFLAG), the National Gay and Lesbian Chamber of Commerce, the National Center for Lesbian Rights, and GLAAD. These alliances gave Marriott access to a large cross section of the LGBT community.

Griffin had hired Bob Witeck of Witeck Communications to work with him on the rollout. Both men were emphatic that working with these LGBT organizations was the best way to gain credibility with their highly influential LGBT members and straight allies. This network of partnerships was key to building Marriott's brand within the LGBT community. As any opportunity or incident came up, Marriott had a preestablished network to get their message out. For example, Marriott could experience a negative incident at one out of its four thousand hotels and immediately craft a response.

With its partnerships buttoned up, Marriott next focused on events. Griffin and Witeck looked at two dozen very popular LGBT Pride events and at the key feeder markets for business and consumer travelers. They identified three key cities in which Marriott would become the title sponsor of the LGBT Pride event: New York, Washington, D.C., and Atlanta. They added Los Angeles later. Marriott's overall strategy was to be out in the general population with an embracing message.

To identify the language to use in its advertising and marketing, Marriott conducted twenty-nine focus groups, from which the researchers pulled key messages: LGBT travelers want to feel welcome, appreciated, and safe. The creative team came up with the tagline "Love Travels" (#LoveTravels), which tested well with focus groups. Marriott encouraged individuals to respond to its ads and to go to Marriott's updated LGBT website and talk about their experiences at Marriott (see Figure 17).

Love Travels has been so successful that it is now the tagline for the other segments that Marriott is trying to reach. According to Bob Witeck, "This was the first time ever that a major marketer designed and presented an LGBT-engaging campaign and rolled it out first and then took that branding to other audiences. LGBT was just the first audience and demographic; Marriott later developed more phases of this campaign for African American and then Latino and Latina audiences—equally effective and with powerful imagery and narratives. But it all began with their LGBT audience."

As the marketing campaign kicked off and continued, Marriott realized it needed to use images and videos of real people in its outreach. So Marriott created campaigns with high-profile LGBT individuals like Jason Collins (the NBA's first openly gay player) and Geena Rocera, a trans model and activist. Marriott wrapped two big buildings in Washington, D.C., with huge graphics of these celebrities and plastered key cities with these images, which exploded on social media and appeared in key mainstream publications.

To assess results, Marriott commissioned customer focus groups for brand preference among LGBT travelers. Before the campaign, Marriott was third or fourth; after the campaign, it was first or second. On the revenue side across the LGBT segment, Marriott tracked $9 million in incremental new income, which captures revenues trackable through disclosed e-mail addresses no matter which channel the buyer ultimately purchased through.

DOMESTIC LUXURY HOTELS: SLS, LAS VEGAS

Today Las Vegas is the number-one destination for LGBT travelers, a stunning reversal for this destination, which didn't register with LGBT travelers before 2006. Las Vegas's luxury hotels played a large role in the turnaround. Michael Bertetto, director of advertising, PR, and social media for the SLS Hotel and Casino, Las Vegas, explains how the transformation happened: "Between *Showgirls* and Liberace, you can argue that Las Vegas was always gay! But in terms of specific market outreach, it all started in 2004, when Luxor Hotel & Casino began reaching out to the LGBT market. Harrah's followed, and then the Convention and Visitors Authority chose to do an LGBT ad buy with the popular What Happens Here, Stays Here campaign in 2006. By 2008 Las Vegas was the number-one most-visited destination in the United States among LGBT travelers."

Las Vegas's first ad creative was not specifically gay, but it worked. Experts usually recommend the opposite. How did that first ad creative come about? Bertetto explains,

At that time, as one of the only openly gay employees at R&R Partners [a consulting firm], I attended advertising creative meetings. Early ad creative (not approved) were with hot, shirtless men. That image was not the brand. What was ultimately created was an offshoot of the ads that reflected the What Happens Here, Stays Here tourism campaign. The debut ad was the lint roller with glitter and eyelashes and that famous tagline. The very first ad for the LGBT market was actually a set of mainstream ads that were overwhelmingly popular, and the destination quickly ran them across all platforms. These were the beauty and magic of Las Vegas ads. We didn't have to create a "gay campaign" with a gay tagline. After those initial ads came new gay-specific ad creative (that relied on imagery), along with a little serendipity. The Paris Las Vegas Hotel relaunched their marketing campaign with Everything Is Sexier in Paris, also created by R&R Partners. For the gay market, the image in that ad was playing cards paired Jack with Jack, Queen with Queen.

Through his experiences, Bertetto learned a valuable lesson: you don't have to have a separate campaign to reach out to the LGBT market. Las Vegas never came out with a "gay campaign." Rather, it performed LGBT-oriented executions of its over-all campaigns that focused on a brand and connected with it in a certain way.

Nonetheless, when preparing to launch Las Vegas's luxury SLS hotel, the executive team evaluated the product with respect to the LGBT market. SLS is a Los Angeles brand, and its parent company was one of the owners of the Abbey (a popular gay bar in West Hollywood, California). "It was never a question of whether we were LGBT-friendly or not," Bertetto says. "LGBT is built into the DNA of SLS, which is a brand that appeals to a younger generation. The millennial generation embraces lesbian, gay, bisexual, and trans friends without question. Our HR policies were in place and employees were aware that we are a gay-friendly establishment. LGBT was part of SLS from the moment we opened our doors. It's different if the product or brand has been around for a while and then it becomes gay-friendly. In that case, you'd have to retrain executive teams, and that starts from top down."

That training can be intense and effective. At Wynn Las Vegas, the HR team invited members of the trans community to talk to executives, who were then predominately males forty years and older. Once the conversation happened, Bertetto says:

> The guys asked some great, deep questions about issues and concerns that trans customers face. If you are a trans person walking on the casino floor, what are your impressions, feelings? This information helped us round out our efforts. Later, when we had a conference with a national HR organization and a middle-aged very straight white man asked about gender-neutral bathrooms, I realized that we walked the walk and talked the talk. For the first time in business settings, people are asking the right questions. It's not a taboo. Now you have the VP of security coming in to make sure staff know the company policies on marriage equality and trans issues.

Because gaming floors can be very macho, testosterone-drenched places, Bertetto offers some tips for marketing a gaming property to LGBT people.

- Gaming is evolving. It's no longer the number-one driver of revenue in Las Vegas, so the LGBT segment is a good customer because they already enjoy the other amenities: dining, shopping, entertainment, and nightlife. For gaming, you're seeing a lot more themed machines, including an Ellen DeGeneres game and a Wonder Woman game with appeal to the LGBT audience. If a gaming floor feels right, people will gamble.
- Creating a welcoming and safe environment comes down to floor employees. LGBT guests will not blame the hotel or brand for stupid customers or guests . . . as long as hotel employees handle a situation correctly.
- Making your stance on key issues clear is also important. For example, recently our security team asked about how to handle customers who are uncomfortable with bathroom use. We told them that they need to tell customers, politely, that our policy is that any person can use the restroom for the gender he or she is presenting.

- Track ROI, and have a dedicated LGBT database. Measure social media engagement. Looking for LGBT dollars is hard unless it is a group that you can track. It's a long-term effort.

See Figure 18 for a good example of a Las Vegas hotel ad appealing to the upscale gay male traveler.

LUXURY HOTELS GLOBALLY: PREFERRED HOTEL GROUP

Preferred Hotels & Resorts (see Figure 19) is the world's largest independent hotel brand, encompassing more than 650 distinctive hotels, resorts, residences, and unique hotel groups across eighty-five countries. We talked with Rick Stiffler, vice president of leisure sales for the Preferred Hotel Group, Preferred Pride (New York City), about Preferred Hotels' entry into the LGBT tourism market and its successes to date.

Stiffler notes that Preferred Hotels & Resorts doesn't own hotels but rather provides marketing, sales, and PR services to hotel owners, operators, and management companies. "I always felt that our independent hotel brands connected naturally to the LGBT audience," he says. "We are unique—not cookie-cutter—properties. I didn't see a lot of luxury hotel product marketing to the LGBT consumer. The competition was in the mid-level hotel range, not five-star. It was more of a given that five-star or five-diamond hotels treat everyone the same. Kimpton Hotels set the way in terms of direct marketing and being forward thinking with the LGBT audience, but I wanted to see more of a luxury product in the space."

How did Stiffler go about implementing his ideas? "In 2010 I gave a presentation at our hotel conference for 150 to 200 people. My presentation was on the color of money and the value of the LGBT travel market. It was the '101' on the LGBT travel segment. Once you toss out some of the big LGBT consumer numbers, it really grabs the attention of the hotel general managers and directors of sales and marketing. The response was so strong that our president agreed to move forward with developing Preferred Pride."

Stiffler explains how the Preferred Pride name came about.

Our campaign doesn't have the word *gay* or a rainbow flag in it. The word *Pride* resonates, so we combined it with Preferred, the company name. I was given a small budget to create this new subbrand called Preferred Pride. We have Preferred Family, Preferred Golf, and Preferred Pride. When we sign new hotels, Preferred Pride is presented as part of what we can offer them. Preferred Pride creates a platform for hotels to reach out to the LGBT segment. Our original goal was 10 to 15 percent hotel participation. We currently have 150 hotels in the program, so it's about 25 percent participation. All of the co-op fees go to marketing, sales, and PR for the program.

Participating hotels create a Preferred Pride rate that travel agents can book, and there is a dedicated site where the hotels can load their rates. Generally, it is the Best Available Rate plus an amenity. The amenity has to be worth at least twenty-five dollars. Some give a free bottle of champagne, a free bottle of wine, or a free breakfast.

How has the program been received? "We marketed to LGBT consumers directly both online and internationally," Stiffler says. "On the travel agent side, we have dedicated collateral that describes the program and what it stands for. Whether you are LGBT, a friend, or an LGBT ally, you can book this Preferred Pride rate. The feedback has been amazing. It was widely embraced by travel agencies but a big education for hotels. PR activity was great. Our story was picked up globally from Russia to Tokyo to Sydney. All that allowed us to measure the success of the program, but we also felt it was simply the right thing to do."

Stiffler cites the following as the most important things that LGBT guests want in a hotel:

- Feeling invited and welcome is important.
- Comfort is important. If a hotel is engaged with the local LGBT community, that is something that makes a guest feel more comfortable.
- Location is important, especially if people are coming for a Pride event or a fun weekend that may involve their visiting gay-popular restaurants and nightlife venues.
- Marketing materials are important. Many LGBT travelers read LGBT publications and notice branding and imagery. They will notice if a hotel is linked to an LGBT charity event.

Stiffler offers the following tips for putting a hotel brand or marketing group on the LGBT map.

1. **Get involved in the local LGBT community.** Know what's going in your own backyard. Get involved with the local LGBT chamber of commerce. Attend LGBT conferences. Some destination marketing campaigns have LGBT outreach, and that is an opportunity to get engaged.

2. **Get involved in local charities.** Give back to the community, which gets you involved and allows you to target the audience that you want at your hotels. Preferred Pride volunteers at Fashion Forward and has donated $300,000 worth of hotel stays over the last four years, targeting an audience that can stay at its hotels. Charity tie-ins allow for great targeting. Preferred Pride and the participating hotels have logos everywhere, and prizes have high visibility.

3. **Advertise.** But do so with LGBT-specific creative executions in all marketing efforts, including ads.

4. **Incorporate LGBT imagery into mainstream advertising and marketing collateral where possible.** Luxury-seeking gays are still reading the *New York Times* and the *Wall Street Journal*. They are not looking at gay media only. Include same-sex couples in your own (internal) corporate imagery, such as hotel catalogs and pieces for sales directors.

5. **Create LGBT content for the market.** Preferred Pride has a blog that talks about what's going on at hotels in the LGBT communities. Reach out to the consumer directly—these efforts have proven to be very popular.

6. **Train your staff and anticipate questions or tricky situations.** There is no substitute for staff training on all parts of the property. The front desk must be trained how to welcome same-sex couples, and the property should have an educated concierge who has information that gay guests may request. Also examine your room setup. Is the room set up for two men or two women (robes, slipper sizes, cosmetics)? Train staff in appropriate language and responses. How do they respond if someone complains about seeing two men or two women kissing by the pool? If you host gay weddings and honeymoons, make sure that your contract language doesn't say "bride and groom."

7. **Assess the success of your campaign using metrics such as revenue, cost, PR, guest-spend levels compared to other markets, length of stay, and return rate.** The LGBT market can be difficult to track. For example, corporate customers can book the Preferred Pride rate without being gay. The marketing may drive consumers to the site, but they may book something else. Despite these challenges, Preferred Pride estimates that it generated close to $1 million in revenue in its first year, and that number increased to $4 million generated from the hotel code.

3L | MEETINGS, CONVENTIONS, AND BUSINESS GROUPS

In the meeting and convention world, many LGBT groups can be found within the SMERF (social, military, educational, religious, and fraternal) market. There are LGBT-related groups for just about everything, from the Gay and Lesbian Association of Doctors and Dentists in London to the International Lesbian, Gay, Bisexual, Trans, and Intersex Association. Wikipedia has an excellent list of LGBT-related organizations and conferences.[19]

In 2007 Jack Ferguson, senior vice president (later president and CEO) of the Philadelphia Convention and Visitors Bureau (CVB), said, "The LGBT convention market is still in its embryonic stage and is developing towards infancy."[20] In 2015 Julie Coker, president and CEO of the Philadelphia CVB, affirmed that LGBT groups are now firmly in the SMERF market, the Out & Equal conference being one of the largest conventions in the United States. Why has this change happened, and what opportunities does it offer?

It used to be more difficult to tap the LGBT meeting, group, and convention market because meeting planners and group organizers (often volunteers) were harder to find and the lack of permanent offices prevented traditional sales calls. Today, however, the web has made these planners visible and easier to reach.

Here are some examples of LGBT groups that travel (and therefore need accommodations and other amenities).

- Out & Equal, which was founded in 1996, brings together employees and experts annually at its Workplace Summit, where attendees learn about current and emerging best practices to ensure greater opportunities and equality for LGBT employees. The annual conference draws more than three thousand people.[21]

- There are more than 180 LGBT choruses throughout the world. GALA Choruses leads the North American LGBT choral movement, and Proud Voices is a group of LGBT choir groups from across Asia. GALA's conventions typically attract about six thousand delegates from 130 choruses who spend five days singing and spending.[22]

- Creating Change, staged by the National LGBTQ Task Force, is the largest annual organizing and skills-building conference for the LGBT community. The five-day conference features more than 250 workshops and training sessions, along with networking opportunities and plenary sessions with nationally known speakers. Attendance can exceed three thousand.[23]

The host city reaps strong economic benefits from hosting LGBT conventions. For example:

- The Los Angeles Tourism and Convention Board reported a $950,000 economic impact to Los Angeles from a recent International Gay and Lesbian Travel Association Convention. Delegates to the three-day convention spent $260,000 at the Hyatt Regency alone.[24]

- Las Vegas is a popular destination for meetings and conventions for all kinds of travelers. The Las Vegas Convention and Visitors Authority (LVCVA) saw the value in the LGBT market and wanted to position the city to earn the business. As Las Vegas entered the LGBT tourism market, the destination sought meeting, group, convention, and large-event opportunities. In recent years the LVCVA recorded booking 85,000 room nights for LGBT groups, which had a non-gaming economic impact of over $25 million.

"Our goal was to educate our hotel partners on the bottom-line value that LGBT meetings and conventions represented, and to share best practices with the sales and management teams in order to provide the best service possible," said Mya Reyes, former LVCVA director of the LGBT market. "As more destinations realize the value of LGBT meetings and conventions, groups will have a larger variety of destinations to choose from and ultimately provide better value to their members," Reyes predicted. (Reyes is now president of the Las Vegas Gay Visitors Bureau.)

3M | MILESTONE CELEBRATION TRAVEL: WEDDINGS, HONEYMOONS, AND OTHER CELEBRATIONS

Hosting small-group celebrations such as birthdays, anniversaries, New Year's Eve parties, and other getaways by groups of LGBT friends is a relatively untapped channel. Many gay men celebrate life's milestones (such as a wedding, anniversary, or a major birthday) with groups of friends in far-flung destinations. Many times they rent large homes in gay-popular resort destinations such as Puerto Vallarta, invite (and often pay for) a dozen or more of their closest friends, hire chefs and drivers, and enjoy a week with their chosen families. Another highly lucrative tourism and hospitality opportunity is the same-sex wedding party. Very often this type of celebration is organized by one of the many same-sex wedding planners that have cropped up over the more than ten years that gay marriage has been legal in Massachusetts and other states. Many existing resorts are the ideal venues for these gatherings, especially resorts that have villas or multi-bedroom suites and kitchen facilities available.

Currently, few suitable resort properties are marketing to these LGBT groups. The challenge is that there is usually one super-organized member of the group who is responsible for the arrangements, and that person isn't necessarily easily identified or reached. *ManAboutWorld* magazine publishes an annually updated service feature each January, "Weddings, Honeymoons + Celebration," which compiles the expert advice of the world's leading LGBT travel, wedding, and honeymoon experts. The feature offers a good way for advertisers to reach gay travelers and their travel consultants.

Before marketing to any small LGBT group, a destination or resort must conduct an audit of certain aspects of their location and hotel property, assessing the gay-friendliness of the destination and the hotel; staff training and sensitivity; and even internal considerations such as whether the hotel includes antidiscrimination HR policies.

Bernadette Smith, founder and president of 14 Stories and the Equality Institute and widely considered the nation's leading same-sex wedding expert, offers some suggestions for determining whether the destination and hotel are truly sensitive to the needs of LGBT wedding groups.

You must know whether the destination is gay-friendly. In this era of increasing acceptance of same-sex relationships, many U.S. and Western gay couples wishing to marry think they can go anywhere in the world to marry, including the most popular wedding destinations, such as Mexico or the Caribbean. However, most travel planners savvy about the LGBT market would never send their clients to Jamaica or Barbados. It's also important to know the legality of gay marriage in your jurisdiction. There are still 179 countries where it is not legal.

Can the hotel ensure privacy? Envision a beach ceremony, which may be on a public beach. Any other hotel guests can be walking the beach (or garden or other outdoor location) where they or even the public can stumble into it. How does the property respond to the question about this scenario? The hotel needs to ensure that guests won't get hecklers. Hotels should be able to answer the question about providing security. The hotel must ensure sensitivity training to the staff. How would a staff member handle one of the guests who may not want to be there (a spouse of an invited guest or a relative who doesn't approve of same-sex marriage) venting to a staff member?

Another consideration for a hotel: often officiants, DJs, and other talent are included in a wedding package. Do they have experience officiating or playing at a same-sex wedding celebration? Are they sensitive to how different same-sex weddings can be from heterosexual weddings and celebrations? Often same-sex couples end up flying in their own officiants and talent at their own cost to avoid negative consequences. A hotel's sensitivity to this would ease the travelers' concerns and decrease unnecessary expenditures.

LGBT tourism and marketing can still stir up controversy, but recent case studies lead us to conclude that tourism and hospitality always win. As public acceptance, laws, business opportunities, and generational attitudes shift toward LGBT equality, the economic upsides far outweigh the short-term drama over any controversy. No boycott or backlash has ever negatively affected any business or destination that has actively courted LGBT travelers.

In 2007 Meryl Levitz, then president and CEO of the Greater Philadelphia Tourism Marketing Corporation (GPTMC), said, "The first question you should ask is, Who might this impact positively and negatively?" She suggested making a list of who might be against you and who might be hurt by a gay tourism program. That advice remains sound.[25]

That said, there is a major difference between then and now: today there are many examples of key destination-marketing organizations, meeting industry associations, large and small businesses, elected officials, funders, and others that rally to the defense of LGBT tourism when controversy arises. For example, when Indiana passed a Religious Freedom Restoration Act in 2015, tourism and meeting officials along with the U.S. Travel Association and Starwood Hotels and Resorts Worldwide (among others) joined forces to have the law amended because it was an assault on fairness and equality and potentially very harmful to their business interests.[26]

The following sections discuss some recent legal and political challenges and how the LGBT travel market has responded.

RELIGIOUS FREEDOM RESTORATION ACTS

Even as LGBT people began achieving civil rights, the tourism and hospitality industry (along with the LGBT community itself) began to confront laws that were being used, proposed, or enacted to allow legal discrimination against LGBT persons. Often called Religious Freedom Restoration Acts, these laws seek to protect businesses from providing a service that is contrary to their religious beliefs. These laws can sanction active discrimination against LGBT persons. Consider these examples:

- Shortly after the U.S. Supreme Court ruling on marriage for same-sex couples, a backlash calling for "religious exemptions" and "religious freedoms" ignited around the country. One example is the case of Kim Davis, a county clerk in Kentucky, who illegally defied the Supreme Court by denying marriage licenses to same-sex couples by saying she was acting "under God's authority." Davis was sent to jail for five days for contempt of court and largely silenced after Pope Francis distanced the Vatican from her stance after she claimed his endorsement.[27]

- More than 29,000 people donated to a crowd-funding campaign to help Memories Pizza stay in business after the owners allegedly had to close their doors amid backlash for saying they would not cater a gay wedding. More than $840,000 was raised, in only four days, to support the Indiana-based business.[28]
- In 2014 *The Guardian* (London) reported: "A Northern Ireland bakery run by devout Christians could face legal action after it refused to make a gay-themed cake depicting the Sesame Street couple Bert and Ernie. Ashers Baking Company published a statement on its website defending its decision to refuse to bake the cake as the slogan above the puppets was in support of gay marriage."[29]

For those who think a cake isn't a big deal, it is a big deal to a gay person denied something so basic. (Think back to the 1960s in the Deep South of the United States, when opponents of civil rights suggested that it shouldn't be a big deal for black people to use their own water fountain.)

But how do hospitality businesses combat Religious Freedom Restoration Acts and other actions that could adversely affect tourism (and are just blatantly discriminatory)? Exactly this challenge confronted the head of New Orleans' destination marketing organization, as the case study explores in detail.

CASE STUDY

COMBATING DISCRIMINATION IN LOUISIANA

In May 2015 the Marriage and Conscience Act was introduced and considered ultimately defeated in Louisiana. Legal experts said that the proposed religious freedom legislation would allow private businesses to refuse to recognize same-sex marriages on the basis of a religious or moral objection.*

When the bill stalled during the legislative process, Louisiana Governor Bobby Jindal issued an executive order that mirrored that house bill. (Jindal later failed in a U.S. presidential bid in which he attempted to position himself as a national leader on religious freedom.) As Jindal left office in 2015, *Newsweek* published an article titled "How Bobby Jindal Broke the Louisiana Economy."† His severely damaged reputation and lack of traction in the 2016 Republican primary process may indicate in part the folly of mixing anti-LGBT discrimination and business. But a more significant factor was the community response against his actions.

Mark C. Romig, president and CEO of the New Orleans Tourism Marketing Corporation, said that a collective effort was forged to invalidate and defeat the governor's executive order. "It was an amazing response from the community, straight and gay, coming out of this area saying to the legislature, no way, this is not appropriate. It helped galvanize our effort."‡

Fortunately, New Orleans already had an antidiscrimination law on the books. Romig said that the city had a strong mayor, Mitchell Joseph "Mitch" Landrieu, who evaluated the threat and jumped right into the argument. "He didn't sit back and watch."

"We started with a strong hand locally, as the tourism and hospitality community already supported LGBT travel," Romig explains. "It supports jobs. We had to make a straightforward business case even though we also knew it was the right thing to do. We had all the right players lined up: the hotels, the restaurants, and the attractions. This little island we call 'NOLA'—we were going to fight Goliath if we had to. We mobilized. The business case is that while NOLA is a minority compared to the state, we had to appeal to the majority. The appeal was that with visitation—whether gay or straight—you are supporting jobs. And it is the right thing to do. We are a very open and welcoming city. What city is going to have a sign at the interstate that says you are not welcome here because of your religion or your sex or any other characteristic?"

Stephen Perry, president and CEO of the New Orleans Convention and Visitors Bureau, made a similar comment: "New Orleans has historically demonstrated itself as one of the most welcoming, open, tolerant, and inviting communities in the world. We are opposed to all legislation that could either limit our freedom of religion for all or that could negatively impact our state's economy and our reputation."§

---

* "New Orleans Welcomes All," www.neworleansonline.com/news/2015/May/hb707.html; Julia O'Donoghue, "Religious Freedom Fight Is Coming to Louisiana," *New Orleans Times-Picayune*, April 3, 2015, www.nola.com/politics/index.ssf/2015/04/religious_freedom_fight_headed.html.

† Stephanie Grace, "How Bobby Jindal Broke the Louisiana Economy," *Newsweek*, June 1, 2015, www.newsweek.com/how-bobby-jindal-broke-louisiana-economy-337999.

‡ Interview with Mark Romig, November 2015.

§ New Orleans CVB press release, "New Orleans Tourism Industry Responds to Louisiana Governor's Executive Order," May 20, 2015, www.neworleansonline.com/pr/releases/releases/XO%20Response%20News%20Release_1.pdf.

DEVELOPING A RESPONSE

Hospitality and tourism businesses can take several steps to develop an effective response to anti-LGBT legislation. An important goal is working in advance to avoid boycotts that might lead any meeting to move to another destination. Here are some examples of the consequences of discriminatory laws on businesses:

- Hotels cannot easily replace large blocks of sold hotel rooms. Even if a large meeting is canceled one year in advance, the chances of filling all those rooms are not good. In essence, the hotel has already put up the "no vacancy" sign, and people have booked somewhere else. The hotel can never recover the lost revenue: an unoccupied hotel room is lost revenue forever.

- Meeting planners get paid once for arranging a meeting—not twice. If a meeting has to be moved as a result of discriminatory laws, they do not get to charge a second time. They can demand a list of welcoming destinations and thus avoid discriminatory destinations forever after. The destination essentially becomes a "do not fly zone" that loses vast opportunities to attract tourists.
- The American Society of Association Executives (ASAE) has a large voice in planning annual conventions. To move one because of internal pressure to avoid a particular destination has a domino effect on that destination, as other associations follow ASAE's lead.

Formulating an effective response requires coordination between the stakeholder groups. In general, convention and visitors bureaus must develop the business case that proves to lobbyists and elected officials that passing discriminatory laws will have negative consequences (as detailed above). In general, the people who work for CVBs and destination-marketing organizations (DMOs) understand the importance of being a welcoming destination regardless of their visitors' political or religious affiliations (or sexual orientation or gender identity).

TIPS FROM THE EXPERTS

DEALING WITH RELIGIOUS FREEDOM RESTORATION ACTS

Charlie Rounds is a cofounder of RSVP Vacations and a pioneer in LGBT travel. He is a lifelong global advocate for human rights and a business leader. Here is his strategy for dealing with Religious Freedom Restoration Acts.

The industry needs to engage experts in large group travel, including conventions and events, to develop a clear path forward to create an effective strategy in stopping future RFAs [religious freedom acts] and dismantling current ones. When a state's hospitality industry has to deal with an inhospitable law, chaos ensues. Bring together hospitality stakeholders—executives from travel companies, convention and visitors bureaus, state tourism organizations, corporate and private meeting planners, and association executives—to create and implement a comprehensive plan to ensure that no traveler is denied hospitality.

What are the business reasons to care about RFAs? To move a meeting of even 500 people from one destination or hotel to another can be incredibly complex and costly to attendees and organizers alike. Attendees have purchased nonrefundable airplane tickets, hotel rooms, and sightseeing trips. Special events have been set up in hard-to-reserve venues. Entertainers have been scheduled. Elevate this to 5,000 or in some cases 50,000 attendees, and you truly have a logistical nightmare.

The industry provides numerous other case studies from which marketing and PR executives can draw important lessons.

1. Fort Lauderdale: Saying the right thing. In 2007 Fort Lauderdale's Mayor Jim Naugle began a very public campaign against the LGBT community. He spoke against LGBT businesses and declared war on the gay community, blaming residents and visitors for Fort Lauderdale's high rate of HIV infection. He also opposed an LGBT library.

Almost ten years later, in an interview about the controversy and its effect on many segments of Fort Lauderdale's tourism industry—notably the family, multicultural, and LGBT tourism markets—Nikki Grossman, president of the Greater Fort Lauderdale Convention and Visitors Bureau, said:

> Ultimately, the right side of that issue prevailed. It was a battle that should never have happened. I was wrongfully credited with taking a hard stand. To me, taking a stand in opposition to what the mayor was saying was one of the easiest things I've ever done. He was dead wrong. There needed to be a voice as loud as his negative voice. I was thrilled and honored to do it. The whole destination was counting on someone to stand out there and counter that loud voice. And his voice did not reflect our destination. We had letters and phone calls from angry people saying they "would not visit your destination because your mayor is homophobic." I had to speak. It had to happen and quickly.
>
> The Broward County Tourism Development Council removed the mayor from the county commission because his comments and intentions did not match Broward County's goals. Mayor Naugle didn't care what the community felt. He felt what he was thinking was so important, and it was necessary to be heard. But there should never have been his voice with those words in this destination because of what the destination has always been. So my advice is, if someone in an elected position or an important position is saying the wrong thing: say the right thing.

2. "So Gay" South Carolina. In 2008 scandal erupted when the state governor's office objected to South Carolina's inclusion in the So Gay international ad campaign in London. The campaign was developed by Out Now for Amro Worldwide, from concept to implementation. The marketing effort comprised posters in the London Underground that featured photographs of well-known landmarks from six U.S. destinations, accompanied by a legend declaring each destination to be "So Gay."

As the Internet and social media started to expand rapidly, images from that campaign captured the media's attention, and controversy quickly ensued, engulfing South Carolina's conservative governor, Mark Sanford. State officials claimed that they were blindsided by the campaign, effectively pinning blame on an experienced ten-year employee of the state Department of Parks, Recreation, and Tourism. The state didn't pay for the ads. Two years later, Sanford, who forced this low-level employee's resignation over the London print ads, resigned after it was found that he'd cheated on his wife with a South American journalist and had left his state for a week and lied about his whereabouts. Unfortunately, attempted discrimination continues in the state, where in 2014 elected officials targeted the University of South Carolina Upstate and the College of Charlestown for encouraging students to read LGBT literature and history.[30]

3. Disney: Driving into the skid. When your car begins to slide over a slippery surface, the best advice is to drive into the skid, which allows the car to right itself and continue on safely. Disney World did exactly that. Perhaps the greatest answer to any conservative group that says, "Traditional family values trump the homosexual agenda," is to cite two events that take place at Walt Disney World Resorts. Arguably the largest travel company synonymous with traditional family values is Walt Disney World Resorts, which is home to princesses, princes, fairy tales, evil queens, and "Gay Days Orlando." After a period marked by an unsure public relationship with the LGBT community, Walt Disney World Resorts now embraces the LGBT community across all its brands.

Eight years before the U.S. Supreme Court ruled in favor of same-sex marriages, Walt Disney World reversed its wedding policy, which at the time discriminated against same-sex couples, in line with an anti-gay Florida marriage law. Starting in 2007, gay couples could buy the company's high-end Fairy Tale Wedding package, which allows them to exchange vows at Disney's theme parks and aboard its cruise ships.[31]

By 2014 Walt Disney Company formed a partnership with Family Outfest, a weeklong event for LGBT families that debuted in Orlando in the summer of 2014. The event's mission is "to celebrate the shared cultural heritage of what all families look like, regardless of who you are, how you identify or whom you love."[32]

TURNING RELIGIOUS CONTROVERSY INTO MARKETING GOLD

As the LGBT travel industry matures and spreads around the world, it will continue to encounter checks against its growth, particularly by representatives of conservative religions. How can you turn religious controversy into a strategy for shifting it to the advantage of the LGBT travel statement?

Rika Jean-François, of ITB Berlin, was invited to do an ITB Academy in Goa, India, at the Goa Travel Market. But an archbishop and a right-wing Hindu group pushed to cancel it, which the organizers did. How did Jean-François turn that challenge into marketing gold? According to Jean-François, "We had a big press conference, which

ENCOUNTER HOMOPHOBIA IN ACCOMMODATIONS?
LAUNCH YOUR OWN!

Even in progressive Western nations, a gay couple can still encounter objections to the simple fact of their sharing a bed in paid accommodations. In larger hotels chains and even in smaller lodging options outside larger cities, gay couples rarely encounter this challenge—thanks in part to the power of TripAdvisor reviews—but in the new sharing economy, the challenge has been reborn.

Matthieu Jost and his same-sex partner encountered this problem when checking into their Airbnb accommodation in Barcelona. The host was uncomfortable with hosting a gay couple. Airbnb, which has strict policies against discrimination by its hosts who offer accommodations, nonetheless cannot police all its listings. According to a CNN article, Jost explained that "the host was not aware he [Jost] and his partner were a gay couple, and the situation prompted them to return home to Paris the next day." The experience led Jost to launch in 2013 Misterbnb, a website providing short-term rentals for gay travelers. Not all the hosts are gay, but they all declare themselves as gay-friendly. The website is now accessed in more than 130 countries, and there are some 33,500 hosts offering accommodations to travelers, which makes Misterbnb the world's largest gay hotelier.* Of course, Misterbnb is much smaller than Airbnb, but it serves as a good example of how to accommodate gay travelers' needs, and it's wise for hotel marketers to take note of this service.

* Bryan Pirolli, "Misterbnb: Gay Travel Revolution Takes on Homestays," CNN.com, December 10, 2015, www .cnn.com/2015/12/10/hotels/misterbnb-gay-lgbt-travel-airbnb.

brought much more publicity than the seminar itself would have drawn had it happened. The pressroom was packed and for two hours journalists asked questions. The scandal was helpful." (For an interview with Rika, see Section 6C.)

DISCUSSION QUESTIONS

1. Explain how LGBT events, festivals, and sporting events can become reliable business drivers.
2. What are some of the ways that destinations embrace their LGBT events to ensure a successful outcome?

3. How can you tailor your product to welcome the LGBT community? If you are unable to implement the ideas in this chapter directly, in what ways can you help indirectly?

4. The cruising industry has lagged behind other tourism and hospitality industries in outreach to the LGBT market. How would you reverse this lag and actively engage the LGBT traveler?

5. What types of things does your business need to consider when hosting an LGBT group, such as a same-sex wedding?

6. How can a marketer effectively turn a controversy into an opportunity?

4

MARKETING YOUR BUSINESS

CHAPTER SUMMARY

This chapter includes the following sections on marketing your business: setting your marketing goals, budget, and staff; getting your advertising history straight; strategies for building an effective marketing campaign; the changing media landscape; great content in context is your foundation; communications, public relations, and media relations; smart press trips; LGBT print advertising and gay-inclusive creative; online and digital marketing; marketing through mobile phone apps; ten tips to keep your LGBT campaign and your destination competitive; and ten classic principles of successful LGBT marketing.

KEY TERMS

marketing
LGBT advertising
homophobia
transphobia
LGBT media
content in context
press trips
gay-inclusive creative
online and digital marketing
three stages of LGBT travel
mobile marketing
LGBT marketing

Guaracino, Jeff, and Salvato, Ed, *Handbook of LGBT Tourism and Hospitality*
dx.doi.org/10.17312/harringtonparkpress/2017.03.hlgbtth.004
© 2017 by Jeff Guaracino and Ed Salvato

Marketing is the activity, set of institutions, and processes for creating, communicating, delivering, and exchanging offerings that have value for customers, clients, partners, and society at large.

—American Marketing Association

Just a decade ago, social media were in their infancy and traditional print advertising was dominant. Since 2010, marketing programs have shifted to a strong emphasis on social media and the web. Jon Allen, owner of Island House in Key West, sums up how marketing has changed in the last decade: "Consumers are now firmly in control of your reputation, especially with TripAdvisor and Yelp. 'Word of Internet' has replaced 'word of mouth.' Marketing is social media. The challenge is to do a good job first and then to drive volume to your website."

In this chapter we present best practices in marketing, expert strategies, and tips for reaching LGBT travelers. Overall, this chapter is a "master class" that presents broad concepts with actionable insights. Because every marketer has different goals and challenges, you will need to tailor a specific marketing plan to your business or product.

Marketers use words and phrases such as *content, going viral, leveraging data, noise, innovation, disruption, social media, influencers, community, apps, mobile, creative, media buying, geo marketing, media relations, stunts, frequency, reach, research, channels, customer relationship management,* and *research.* In marketing to the LGBT segment, more words have to be added to the conversation: *stereotypes, pandering, audience,* and *authenticity,* to name just a few.

Let's break it all down to help you get your marketing plan started.

4A | SETTING YOUR MARKETING GOALS, BUDGET, AND STAFF

In creating a marketing plan, you need a laser-focused vision and strategy to steer your efforts. Begin with a thorough assessment of your goals:

- What do you want to achieve? How will you get there?
- How will you measure the results of your marketing program?
- How does the LGBT segment fit into the overall marketing program, or are you crafting a stand-alone program specifically for LGBT travelers?
- Who are your customers?

- What are the investment and expected financial return?
- Who needs to buy in and who might opt out?
- What are the time line and budget?

SETTING AND WORKING WITH A BUDGET

Every organization has limited budgets, human resources, and time. Decisions must be made to achieve the highest return on investment, which means that you may choose to market to a smaller segment within the LGBT market. For example, you might focus your campaign on people of a certain gender, age range, or income.

There is no single industry budget standard. Marketing budgets vary widely from organization to organization and from department to department. Set your own budget, and make a commitment to it. Larger LGBT destination campaigns are often funded around the $1 million mark annually, but bigger isn't necessarily better. Smarter is better.

Campaigns require sustained investment over time to develop, maintain, or increase your LGBT market share. One way to help set your budget is to turn to Rivendell's "Gay Press Report." To produce the report, Rivendell Media collects all the gay and lesbian publications in the United States, measures the numbers and scope of the advertising therein, and analyzes its content. Changes and categories are tracked over time, and comparisons made across products and industries. Rivendell also produces a "Competitive Tracking Report" that can provide insight into competitive spending within a category. This report charts the rise in a travel product's popularity and the correlation to ad spending.

INVESTMENTS IN HUMAN CAPITAL

The human capital dedicated to marketing to the LGBT segment is an internal decision that varies by company. You can use your internal team, turn to expert consultants, or use a mixture of the two. Some companies have dedicated a specific person

---

TIP!

If you are focusing your marketing efforts on particular L, G, B, or T groups, you should take steps to be inclusive and respectful of the larger LGBT community. Consider employment policies or alignments with LGBT nonprofits to balance a marketing effort aimed at specific type of customer. Focus on now and the future. Your best customers might be future customers, so always eye the new markets within the LGBT segment to increase revenue. (For more details on the various segments, see Chapter 2).

to the LGBT market. That said, as quickly as the industry adds LGBT market directors (for example, in Fort Lauderdale, Florida, and at Belmond hotels), other parts of the industry eliminate their LGBT-dedicated sales and marketing positions.

Ultimately, the individual company or organization must deploy the human resources that best fit its structure and goals. Successful companies, however, dedicate specific people, budgets, and time to the LGBT segment and to the institutionalization of LGBT marketing efforts. The latter is particularly important. Time and time again, the LGBT marketing campaign has been created or led by one person, and when that individual leaves the company, the program ends. If the knowledge and operations haven't been institutionalized, the company is susceptible to falling behind in its efforts and losing potential revenues. How you execute a marketing program will change over time as technology advances and as people shift their behaviors, attitudes, and purchasing patterns.

4B | GETTING YOUR ADVERTISING HISTORY STRAIGHT

Whether you are updating your current advertising campaign or you are just starting out, arm yourself with research on the best and the worst of LGBT advertising. Equipped with the facts and the right creative team, you or your advertising agency will be able to build on earlier successes by learning from other companies' mistakes.

To brush up on LGBT advertising history, firsts, and mistakes, check out the online chronicle of LGBT advertising creative at AdRespect.org. Its founder, Mike Wilke, a business journalist and the founder of the Commercial Closet Association, created AdRespect to work with the advertising industry, creative agencies, and marketers to provide information about representations of diversity, gender identity and expression, and sexual orientation in advertising; his goal was to help businesses get results. In addition, AdRepect's innovative LGBT-Awareness Advertising Training Program presents lesbian, gay, bisexual, and transgender issues in advertising and an educational platform about homophobia, transphobia, LGBT stereotypes, humor, and diversity inclusion. It offers best practices for avoiding mistakes, as well as creative approaches for planning and designing inclusive commercials.

An *Ad Week* journalist, Robert Klara, and Stuart Elliott, a former *New York Times* advertising columnist, are perhaps the two best-known experts on advertising to the LGBT community. Their columns, research, and insights are a must-read for any marketer developing advertising to reach LGBT travelers. You can find their work online at *Ad Week* and in the *New York Times* archives.

Though LGBT advertising might be considered a hot trend, Klara points out that advertising to gay consumers is almost one hundred years old: "After years of baby steps toward LGBT consumers, who represent an estimated $790 billion in spending power, brands like Crate & Barrel, American Airlines, and even Bridgestone Tires have brought their marketing out of the closet, picturing same-sex couples that are unquestionably more than just friends. While it may seem like such ads rode a cultural wave of gay acceptance that began with *Will & Grace* and crested with *Glee,* it is actually a trend that was decades in the making."[1]

Klara points out that the advertising industry has a decades-long history of marketing to LGBT consumers. Campaigns have evolved over time, going from subtle to overt and leveraging "out" celebrities to sell the product:

> A look back through advertising's dusty annals reveals images of startlingly frank male-on-male intimacy dating back to the early 20th century. In fact, images of cherub-faced frat boys and muscled-up gods as well as even strategic bits of nudity—all key ingredients of contemporary marketing targeted to gay men—pop up as early as the 1920s in such mainstream publications as *Life, Collier's* and *The Saturday Evening Post.* Some of the images are eyebrow-raisers even by today's standards. The images tend to be ambiguous—and in many cases, furtive and inadvertent—but their presence is undeniable.[2]

In writing about the top-five most significant changes in advertising over the last twenty-five years, Stuart Elliott points to the rise of diversity marketing as one of the top changes: "As America has come to resemble the 'gorgeous mosaic' of David N. Dinkins, advertisers responded—slowly at first, certainly—with inclusive, multicultural campaigns. . . . And as same-sex marriage becomes more prevalent and accepted, Madison Avenue is running ads with gay, lesbian, bisexual, and transgender consumers in mainstream media, not only in media aimed at this market."[3]

Klara concludes:

> While many early out-gay ads were "extraordinary, high quality" creative, they also tended to be "stereotypical and pandering," notes Gary Hicks, professor of mass communications at Southern Illinois University. They could also be downright silly. Hicks recalls a Budweiser ad picturing a guy reaching into the fridge for a beer with the caption "Another one's coming out." Another ad, also for Bud, shows a coffee table strewn with beer bottles, caps intact, with the line "Tops and Bottles." This form of coded messaging may have resonated loud and clear to gay audiences, but Hicks notes it's also patronizing.[4]

4C | STRATEGIES FOR BUILDING AN EFFECTIVE MARKETING CAMPAIGN

David Jefferys is president of Altus Agency, a respected Philadelphia-based marketing agency and an expert in LGBT marketing. Altus worked with Visit Philadelphia to develop the groundbreaking advertising program Philadelphia Get Your History Straight and Your Nightlife Gay. Altus Agency produces the "Navigaytour," which markets itself as "The Ultimate LGBT Travel Resource Guide."[5]

To build a successful campaign, Jefferys recommends multiple approaches to your target customer as part of an integrated tactical marketing campaign. Here are Jefferys's recommended best practices.

1. **Word of mouth surpasses all other aspects of paid or unpaid advertising.** Before spending money on marketing, make sure your product is worthy of telling a friend about.

2. **People dream in print.** Print does a heavy lift with a headline, image, body copy, signature, call to action, or offer—or any combination of these. Good creative in print produces good public relations. The most effective mobile ads include the best of print ads along with the interactivity of digital ads.

3. **Video adds motion, sound, words, and effects that stimulate the senses.** With video you can tell a story. Like print, video has a high pass-along rate.

4. **Social media offer a sophisticated advertising management system to zero in on a customer and hit a bull's-eye.** Make an emotional connection on social media with a strong offer.

5. **Blogs work.** Blogs are online, and often objective, third-party endorsements. It is worth your time to invest in getting your content and offers to bloggers. Blogging on your own site or social page will create even more engagement. Engagement builds loyalty.

6. **There is no substitute for smart media buying.** Programmatic media buying can cut your budget by as much as 30 percent. It is essentially buying specific audiences using boatloads of data to match the right ad, the right person, and the right time.

7. **Branch out to new forms of marketing and advertising.** Media are changing constantly. Increasing popular is the "advertorial," in which you write a story about the offer with an adjacent ad placement that gives readers the ability to click and buy instantly.

8. **Combine social and e-marketing for stimulus and response.** A bounce page or landing page allows you to capture basic audience information. You can host a bounce page on your own website and on other websites. For example, if you

place an ad on Facebook and the audience likes it, you then capture their information on a bounce page and send them an e-mail.

9. **PR is infinitely adjustable.** Expand and contract your PR budget or efforts as needed. A public relations strategy with a witty advertising campaign along with smart ad buys can pull the entire campaign together.

10. **Look for dashboards that will handle all your data and measure your campaign.** Focus on improving (or eliminating) the underperforming parts of the campaign.

4D | THE CHANGING MEDIA LANDSCAPE: THE RISE, FALL, AND RISE OF LGBT PUBLICATIONS

4 C

4 D

The LGBT community was ignored or vilified by the mainstream media through the 1960s, 1970s, and 1980s—and even beyond. This biased coverage or lack of coverage gave birth to the LGBT media industry. Strong, authoritative, and influential local print publications and national publications were born. Print became the primary source for LGBT news, events, and even for meeting other LGBT people.

With the rise of the Internet in the late 1990s came news and community sites like PlanetOut, Gay.com, and Gay.net. Today there are still many local print publications, including *Gay City News, Philadelphia Gay News,* and *Windy City Times.* Their online platforms reach many more readers globally. Recent media consolidation has seen iconic news brands being absorbed into conglomerates such as Here Media, which publishes *Out* magazine, the *Advocate* magazine, OutTraveler.com, and SheWired.

LGBT media continue to evolve. Print remains strong as it expands its online presence. Digital technology (like apps and Apple's newest devices), combined with self-selected, more fragmented audiences, has led to innovative multiple-platform, multiple-content LGBT media companies. Solo ventures are forging smart partnerships, harnessing strong editorial voices and a significant number of followers for such travel content as *ManAboutWorld* and GayCities.

LGBT-specific media are not dying or completely dissolving into mainstream media. In fact, LGBT-specific content is expanding in new ways, presenting new opportunities for marketers and media buyers. Consider these examples:

• Multimedia Platforms Inc. is a multimedia technology and publishing company that integrates print media, social media, and related online platforms to deliver information and advertising to an LGBT population of 7.5 million readers. This new generation of LGBT media delivers both quality news and entertainment information via a variety of platforms. In 2015 Multimedia Platforms acquired Columbia FunMap, Inc., a thirty-three-year-old LGBT travel and leisure publishing company, bringing together print newspapers, online content, and guide maps.

- Q.Digital publishes GayCities, an online consumer-sourced travel guide; Queerty, a news and pop culture site; the Bilerico Project, a group of LGBT bloggers; Dragaholic; and LGBTQ Nation, a news site.

- The Gay Ad Network describes itself as "the world's largest advertising marketplace for connecting advertisers with gay consumers worldwide. We offer a complete LGBT digital advertising solution." Clients purchase ads, including targeted ads, that appear across various LGBT sites in the network.

- *ManAboutWorld* publishes six regular issues and four themed issues annually that provide expanded advertising and native content opportunities (Weddings, Honeymoons + Celebrations, Tours & Cruises, Summer Getaways, and LGBT Business Travel). Digital-native *ManAboutWorld* is the first gay travel magazine created specifically for iPads, iPhones, and Android devices.

- Towleroad is a trusted online news source with information on a range of topics from politics and pop culture to music and travel. You can find Towleroad online and through social media channels.

- *Passport* magazine is one of several luxury LGBT travel print publications. *Passport* also features an online version and a mobile version, and it sponsors a consumer expo.

"LGBT media is becoming a game changer," says Bobby Blair, chairman of Multimedia Platforms. "We work with national brands directly, ranging from W Hotel to Nissan and Mercedes. It is not an advertising buy; we tell advertisers you can't just throw an ad in a magazine and assume that people will come running. They have to be engaged. Our clients have to show up at Pride events. They have to show support and be there. When the gay and lesbian community see that this company is supportive of social change and this company wants to be a part of the community, then, in return, advertisers get an exponential return on the investment."

TIPS FROM THE EXPERTS

THE CHANGING MEDIA LANDSCAPE

Alan Beck is an LGBT tourism and hospitality media expert specializing in advertising, sales, and publishing. He has forty years of experience in advertising sales, including the production of maps and brochures. For twenty-five years he led and later owned Columbia FunMaps, a respected guide to travel destinations. He understands the changing attitudes of consumers and advertisers, as well as the evolution of the advertising channels available to reach the LGBT visitor.

FIGURE 1 VISIT BRITAIN EXTENDS AN INVITATION TO GAY MEN.

Visit Britain's Love Is Great campaign depicts a range of models, including same-sex couples, both male and female as well as mixed-race, underscoring Great Britain's celebration of diversity.

FIGURE 2 VISIT BRITAIN EXTENDS AN INVITATION TO LESBIANS.

It's very important to use lesbian ads in lesbian publications. If you use gay men, heterosexual couples, or straight women, your message will not resonate much at all. This ad originally appeared in *Curve* magazine, the most popular lesbian magazine in the United States.

FIGURE 3 FORT LAUDERDALE MARKETS THE BEST OF THE DESTINATION.

This is a great example of Nikki Grossman's philosophy of putting yourself "out there" as a destination: multiracial, buff gay men surrounding and even genuflecting to a drag mermaid! All the while they are showcasing some of the best of the destination, including sun and sand.

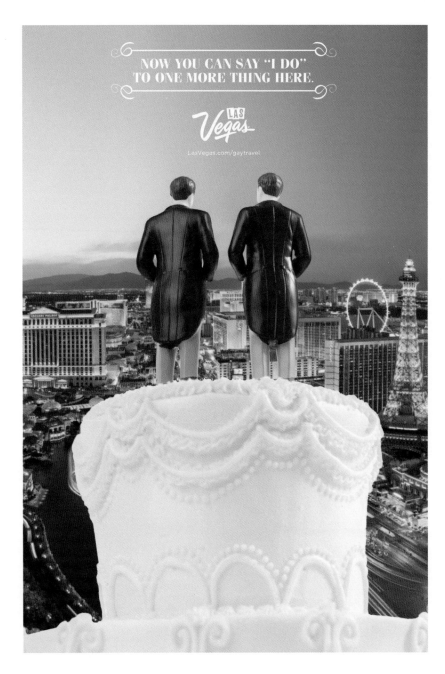

FIGURE 4 SAYING "I DO" LAS VEGAS.

This ad plays to Las Vegas's reputation as a destination where LGBT visitors can pretty much do anything, including saying, "I do." It was released to capitalize on Nevada's law allowing same-sex marriage (before it was available nationally).

FIGURE 5 FORT LAUDERDALE USES REAL LESBIANS IN ITS ADS.

This ad perfectly illustrates *Curve* magazine editor Merryn Johns's suggestion that advertisers show real lesbians —not stock models or evidently heterosexual women—in ads. As in so many other ways, Fort Lauderdale displays best practices in this space.

Win an ultimate lesbian weekend city break!

Introduced by Stockholm's Leading Ladies

Photo by: Yanan Li

Our cool capital city is well known for its super hot girls and thriving lesbian scene, so we've tracked down this smorgasbord of local gay gals to give you an insight into the diverse array of things to do over a weekend in Stockholm. From an action-packed outdoor adventure, to a designer shop fest, art gallery marathon or non-stop party – there's a Stockholm weekend to suit.

ENTER CONTEST >

Our media partners

 DIVA

Lipstick Ladies

FIGURE 6 STOCKHOLM'S LEADING LADIES.

Many destinations market to the overall LGBT market, but Out Now Global Consulting created the successful Stockholm's Leading Ladies campaign targeting the U.K. lesbian market. The campaign also included media partnerships and other tactics that specifically targeted gay women in the United Kingdom.

FIGURE 7 FORT LAUDERDALE COURTS THE TRANS TRAVELER.

Everyone talks about LGBT travel, but very few marketers actively seek the trans traveler. Fort Lauderdale puts the T in LGBT travel through a number of efforts, including this ad— among the first to use real trans travelers in a campaign.

FIGURE 8 GAYGERMANY—100% SO YOU.

Out Now Global worked with VisitBerlin and Lufthansa to create the 100% GayGermany online campaign with a website that asked site visitors to upload short videos and explain why they think GayGermany is "100% so you." Free campaigns targeting LGBT travelers can be very successful as long as they are supported by appropriate online and social promotion.

FIGURE 9 PINK PILLOW BERLIN COLLECTION.

The Pink Pillow Berlin Collection is a group of gay-friendly hotels in Berlin. Out Now created a successful collaboration between Pink Pillow and VisitBerlin (the city's destination marketing organization) that included several elements, such as this off-line event. The LGBT market is high-touch and values in-person events.

FIGURE 10 BORGATA BOASTS ITS 100% SCORE ON THE
CORPORATE EQUALITY INDEX.

Here Borgata displays its pride in receiving a perfect score
of 100 percent on the Human Rights Campaign's Corporate
Equality Index, which is a way for a corporation to telegraph
its acceptance of diversity.

FIGURE 11   UNITED AIRLINES: OPENLY AND PROUDLY LGBT-FRIENDLY.

This ad uses marriage equality, an important freedom won across
the United States in 2015, to reflect United Airlines' overall campaign
to be LGBT-friendly.

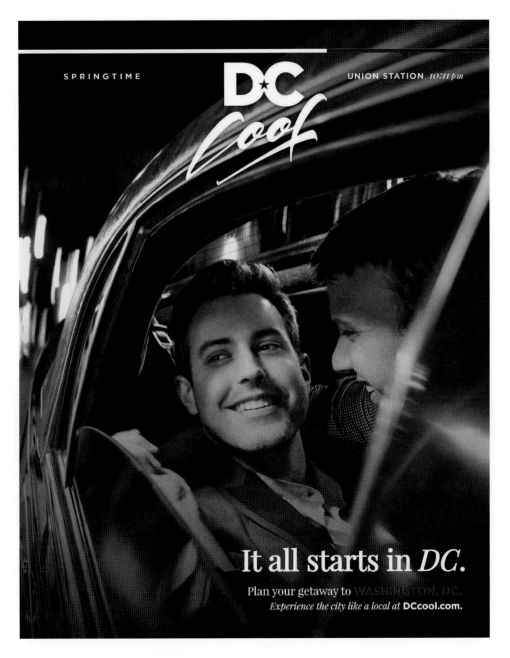

FIGURE 12 IT ALL STARTS IN DC.

Destination DC created a campaign depicting a dressed-up, sophisticated-looking couple enjoying a fun time in the city. Using a gay couple in what appears to be a luxury car with a black-and-white treatment underscores the concept of "cool" that DC promotes. This ad helps the district in general grow beyond its stodgy reputation as "the nation's capital."

fun.free.fabulous.

TEL AVIV GAY VIBE

FIGURE 13 TEL AVIV GAY VIBE.

Tel Aviv promotes its people and its beaches with a gay twist (a drag queen, gay men, and lesbians) and more subtly its freedoms. Where else in the Middle East (or even in Israel) can you feel free to be your fabulous self other than Tel Aviv?

FIGURE 14 AZAMARA CLUB CRUISES USES AN LGBT BOOKING CODE.

The cruise industry has been slow to market directly to LGBT travelers, instead relying on tour operators like Atlantis to market their charters. Here is one of the few mainstream cruise ads that we found. One curious thing: the hashtag is coincidentally very similar to that of Marriott's very successful #LoveTravels campaign.

**We'd like to be your domestic partner.
International, too.**

Every year thousands of LGBT travelers choose Alaska to fly them
to Pride events, all across the country. And every year they save
thousands of dollars with unique LGBT discount codes. But why
stop at the border? As Pride grows around the globe, so does
our commitment to get you there. Check for savings to all your
favorite LGBT events and destinations, like Seattle, Palm Springs
and Puerto Vallarta at **alaskaair.com/gaytravel.**

10%OFF*
SELECT LGBT
EVENTS

*Terms apply. See site for details.

Alaska

CALLING ALL EXPLORERS™

FIGURE 15 ALASKA AIRLINES IS "CALLING ALL EXPLORERS."

Alaska Airlines has been assertive in the LGBT space.
Here's an ad promoting domestic and international
travel during Gay Pride. It is logical to promote during
Pride, but it's wise to note that many other organizations
are promoting around Pride too, so it can be hard to cut
through the clutter.

FIGURE 16 THE PORTER AIRLINES MASCOT.

This cute little guy is Porter Airlines' mascot. Here he welcomes passengers onto a rainbow carpet to wordlessly show Porter's support of Gay Pride.

FIGURE 17 MARRIOTT HOTELS: #LOVETRAVELS.

The Marriott approach was designed to highlight the customer's voice, impressions, and aspirations. Marriott encouraged LGBT travelers to share their own images and experiences, to visit and engage with Marriott's updated LGBT website, and to share how their own LoveTravels. This particular image shows a pair of newlyweds, George and Sean, just after being married by Ross Mathews on the #LoveTravels float during the 2015 Capital Pride Parade.

(Photo credit: Tony Valadez Photography)

FIGURE 18 LUXOR LAS VEGAS APPEALS TO THE UPSCALE TRAVELER.

Here the Las Vegas hotel promotes itself as a luxurious option for gay travelers, depicting well-dressed men rather than the more typical shirtless figures prevalent in so many ads in this space.

FIGURE 19 PREFERRED HOTELS OFFERS AN UPSCALE LGBT EXPERIENCE.

This elegant advertisement was produce by Rick Stiffler, a marketing executive at Preferred Hotels, who saw an opportunity in the LGBT space. With little budget he produced this ad, which includes him and a friend instead of paid models.

FIGURE 20 THAILAND: "GO THAI, BE FREE."

Thailand is the only national destination marketer in all of Asia that reaches out to LGBT travelers. Its tagline, "Go Thai, Be Free," explicitly tells LGBT visitors that they will be welcome and accepted. The pictures are very inviting.

FIGURE 21 BRAZIL'S NATIONAL FAMILY DAY.

This colorful ad about national family day shows how even in Brazil the definition of family is expanding.

FIGURE 22 ITB'S GAY & LESBIAN TRAVEL PAVILION:
LONG LIVE DIVERSITY!

ITB's Gay & Lesbian Travel Pavilion presents the world's
largest range of LGBT tourism products at any trade fair.
ITB has grown every year since 2010.

Beck summarizes the changing media landscape as follows:

- Distribution in print is expensive and time-consuming, but it remains a foundation of LGBT campaigns.
- A print strategy should be tied to getting eyeballs to the Internet. Marketers should buy media with print and online sales packages.
- Once print gets the consumer online, then social media networks carry the conversation. The audience reacts and shares.
- Technology has driven change. Printed maps are helpful when tourists have reached their destination.
- Hotels' advertising strategy has changed. The hotel industry has shifted from a branding strategy to a retail strategy. Hotels appear to have lost interest in print ads and are going digital to reach the audience and sell rooms.
- The meeting ground for LGBT people has shifted from the bar to the mobile phone. As a result, LGBT-owned businesses like bars and clubs have lost revenue. Lost revenues affect gay bars' ability to advertise. New advertisers are casinos, the car industry, and the retail industry.

4E | GREAT CONTENT IN CONTEXT IS YOUR FOUNDATION

Every effective marketing campaign starts with two key components of content: (1) well-written, well-researched copy, and (2) smart, compelling photos or videos (or both) that tell a story. Funny, sexy, sassy, authentic, inspiring: content can and should be all these things.

THE VALUE OF AUTHENTICITY

Travelers are smart and informed consumers, and the recent focus on authenticity has driven a shift in marketing. By *authenticity* we mean relevant content in a relevant context that consumers value. In its quest for authenticity, today's content is less saleslike. Instead, it is more personal and appeals to travelers' passions. Authentic content is delivered at the right time and in the right place. Done well, its increases awareness and loyalty and possibly drives a sale. Done poorly, it risks alienating potential customers.

CONTENT IN CONSUMERS' HANDS

Increasingly, content is in the hands of powerful consumers. In fact, some marketing campaigns rely on crowdsourcing of content and images. Thanks to the accessibility of online review sites like TripAdvisor, consumer-generated reviews are highly influential content that can either reinforce your marketing claims or warn potential consumers of false advertising, inflated claims, or negative experiences with your product.

USING CONTENT TO COMMUNICATE YOUR BRAND PROMISE

The key to effectively communicating your brand promise to LGBT travelers is to determine how to showcase your product or travel experience. It is your content that develops, captures, and reinforces this marketing plan. *ManAboutWorld*'s experiences offer a valuable case study (see the accompanying sidebar).

CASE STUDY

MANABOUTWORLD'S CONTENT PARTNERSHIPS

Billy Kolber, an expert in gay travel content, launched *Out&About* in 1992 and is the cofounder and publisher of *ManAboutWorld* magazine. At *ManAbout-World*, Kolber has been creating content partnerships with some of the world's savviest travel marketers.

Kolber believes that the success of marketing content depends on how well it serves the end user: the LGBT traveler. Magazines and guides continue to play an important role in travel storytelling. Unbound by the constraints of the two-dimensional printed page, stories and guides on a mobile platform reach travelers where they live (on their phones and tablets). They also captivate and inspire travelers in new ways through video, photographs, and animations.

NYC & Company was looking for new ways to entice visitors to New York City's outer boroughs—those beyond Manhattan. To accomplish this goal, the organization forged a content partnership with *ManAboutWorld* to develop a new bike guide to New York City. LGBT NYC by Bike aligned readers' interests—neighborhood exploration, local discoveries, and efficient transportation—with NYC & Company's marketing goals: to increase bike-share usage, to promote Brooklyn and Queens as travel destinations, and to provide an authentic outreach to LGBT visitors.

LGBT NYC by Bike contains pictures, video, words, and maps. The guide is organized by neighborhood and provides travel-time estimates for biking from each neighborhood to every other one in the guide, which includes the "gay-est" CitiBike stations in Manhattan, Brooklyn, and Queens. *ManAboutWorld*'s

---

and NYCgo.com's mobile platforms allow readers to link directly to the Citi-Bike app for more information, to Google Maps for turn-by-turn navigation tailored to bike riders, and to the websites of hundreds of points of interest.

4F | COMMUNICATIONS, PUBLIC RELATIONS, AND MEDIA RELATIONS

Communications, public relations, and media relations are the essential foundation of any successful LGBT campaign. Communications can amplify a well-developed campaign. To understand and market to LGBT travelers, communications professionals must be aware of the nuances within the community, understand the micro- and macro-cultures, and play to the media's need to cover this newsy market in new ways. Communications pros must be agile, creative, and flexible.

The time has passed to simply announce that your client or product is "gay-friendly" or that it now has an LGBT microsite. What makes it different, innovative, better? A sophisticated and effective communications program understands the relationship between the gay and straight communities, the media and the product.

Has the marketing paradigm shifted? It used to be that the advertising and the media buy drove the campaign. Today, especially in LGBT marketing, the key drivers are public relations, community engagement, and social media; advertising and the media buy extend the invitation. The gatekeepers are no longer simply editors and reporters. Today's marketers go directly to consumers, and a PR specialist shapes that narrative and manages the reputation of the company and its products.

What are the qualities of effective PR professionals?

- They know the product, they know the media, and they know how to communicate effectively. There is no substitute for developing an ever-increasing number of media contacts.
- Good PR professionals take a smart story and connect it to the right media. Unlike advertising, which is usually geographically limited, PR is immediately global, thanks to the power of the Internet and social media.
- Their pitches are both timely and tailored. They are ever vigilant for opportunities to spread the message.
- More than ever, PR professionals are available and responsive 24/7. (PR crises and opportunities occur frequently. When was the last time you heard of an advertising emergency?) Exceptional PR professionals foster the intersection of events, marketing, media relations, social media, and advertising.

4G | SMART PRESS TRIPS

Sponsoring a press trip is an investment with an expected (and, we hope, high) ROI. Ideally, press trips align the interests of travel promoters, travel journalists, and travelers. Earned media from press trips is one of the most effective tactics of any campaign because of the media's authoritative and trusted voice. People believe what the media say (or do not say) about a travel experience. Clearly knowing and communicating why you're hosting a press trip is essential to the success of your LGBT campaign. Note, however, that a press trip cannot take the place of a complete marketing campaign.

The following are our top tips for successful press trips. Download the complete guide to press trips at www.LGBTexpert.com.

1. **Whom you invite is an important strategic decision.** Consider asking the industry's best, most professional editors and journalists for recommendations on the best journalists to invite. You will also discover that there are nonproductive "writers" to avoid.

2. **Invite a broad-based but professional group of journalists.** Include content editors and providers for print and digital-native tablet magazines, newspapers, websites, blogs, e-newsletters, and guidebooks. Social media influencers often have styles and priorities that are very different from those of more traditional journalists, but social media experts can be very effective with word of mouth.

3. **Support journalists' associations.** Join the National Lesbian and Gay Journalists Association (NLGJA) or other associations for journalists (gay and straight), which will help you cultivate relationships with LGBT journalists who may work for mainstream or LGBT media.

4. **Guests can be a distraction on many press trips, but there are exceptions.** For destinations or travel experiences not known to be gay welcoming, it can be helpful for your invited media member to have a same-sex guest. Otherwise, a solo gay media rep is only "theoretically" gay.

5. **Timing your trip for events like LGBT Pride or destination-defining events is a best practice.** Shoulder and off-season trips often miss the excitement of a destination. Still, LGBT travelers frequently plan to travel outside school holidays to avoid crowds of heterosexual families. Also, the timing of the press trip depends on the length of lead time your invited media require. Longer-lead journalists may not publish a story for six months or a year. Bloggers or online media outlets may publish in real time or with very short lead times.

6. **Resist pressure from stakeholders** to include venues or activities that are related to other niches and not the LGBT media's interest or audience, particularly if those other venues or activities take time away from core activities such as exploring the gay neighborhood and nightlife.

7. **Keep the gay in the gay press trip.** LGBT events, LGBT venues, LGBT nightlife must be factored in because gays love meeting other gays. Invite local LGBT leaders, personalities, and businesspeople to join the group for meals. Include nightlife options for your LGBT participants, but if they're out at a bar until 2 A.M., don't expect them to show up bright-eyed for an 8 A.M. hotel site inspection

8. **Hire a knowledgeable expert to interpret the culture and history of the city through the lens of a queer person.** For example, engage an LGBT guide who can point out hidden queer angles to paintings in your fine arts museum.

9. **Support the LGBT media (with advertising or other marketing partnerships) that you expect to support your travel product with editorial.** This is a win-win situation for both parties.

4H | LGBT PRINT ADVERTISING AND GAY-INCLUSIVE CREATIVE

4G

4H

Merryn Johns, editor in chief of *Curve,* the best-selling lesbian magazine in the United States, says, "Advertisers don't want to let it go." By it she means the printed word. People seek out magazines, newspapers, and other printed brochures and guides. Print is not dead; the challenge is how to use a print buy to support an overall marketing campaign. Mark Segal, publisher of the award-winning *Philadelphia Gay News,* one of the oldest LGBT newspapers in the United States, describes the influence and importance of LGBT newspapers:

LGBT newspapers offer authoritative news coverage by professional and award-winning journalists who are covering the issues of most importance to the local LGBT communities. Local LGBT newspapers are impactful and influential. They are also good resources for marketers to better understand a particular area. What is important to the local LGBT community? The local sales force of the LGBT newspaper can also be a good connector to other LGBT organizations or events in which you might want to be present (such as an annual LGBT toy drive or a Pride event).

Local LGBT newspapers are powerful advertising vehicles and should be the launching pad and foundation of any LGBT tourism marketing campaign. Print demonstrates that you are committed to the market. Print gives you more space to present your story.

Digital advertising with banner ads and mobile ads are by their very nature "transactional"—you want the person to do something right then and there. Print advertising consistently over time in local LGBT newspapers can be a powerful relationship builder with the paper's readers. LGBT newspapers reach a cross-section of the community, giving your message a reach that most other vehicles can't offer. The online component to the print is essential to reaching more people online. Print provides more opportunity to showcase your company's commitment to workforce equality or to make a stand with the community, such as during Gay Pride Month.[6]

Great print creative can drive word of mouth, publicity, and social buzz. There are many examples of smart creative that are humorous, highly connected to the LGBT audience, and timed to appear in the media at just the right moment.

Here's a good example. Paris Las Vegas was looking to stand out. Paris is on the Strip and its main theme is romantic. But, to boost occupancy, the hotel and casino wanted to be the "sexy" Las Vegas property. The Everything's Sexier in Paris print ads were funny, spoke to the audience, and made a statement. Seemingly everyone noticed them and the Paris Las Vegas Hotel.[7] Michael Bertetto, previously with R&R Partners, the agency on record for the Las Vegas Convention and Visitors Authority, explains how the Paris Las Vegas Hotel created a gay version of the Everything's Sexier in Paris ad campaign using pairs of jacks and queens in gay publications, instead of the jack and queen seen in mainstream media. This variation remained consistent with the overall marketing campaign.[8]

Stuart Elliott of the *New York Times* wrote about a new trend in a column headed, "Commercials with a Gay Emphasis Are Moving to Mainstream Media." His story focused on an Expedia television commercial aimed at the LGBT market. Expedia's ad appeared not only on the Logo television network, which is geared toward the LGBT audience, but also on mainstream networks, including MSNBC.

Stuart wrote:

For the last two or three decades, such ads were usually aimed at L.G.B.T. consumers, placed in media those consumers watch and read, and then supplemented with tactics that included event marketing like floats in Pride Month parades. . . . Recently, however, L.G.B.T. ads have been getting broader exposure. While targeted media and events remain part of the game plan, they are also running in mainstream media that, in addition to general cable channels, include magazines like *Family Circle,* newspapers like *The New York Times* and social media like Facebook, Tumblr, Twitter, and YouTube. One goal is to reach families, friends, and straight allies of L.G.B.T. consumers.[9]

The travel industry pioneered advertising to LGBT people in mainstream media outlets. Nearly a decade before the Expedia ads, Orbitz and the Greater Philadelphia Tourism Marketing Corporation (now Visit Philadelphia) forged a deal that aired Philadelphia's groundbreaking Pen Pals commercial to mainstream networks in major markets. Key West, Florida, aired some of the first gay television commercials for a destination, Out Before It Was In, on mainstream stations.

Increasingly, non–travel industry brands, such as J.C. Penney and Campbell's Soup, have used gay-inclusive ads on broadcast television. According to Bob Witeck of Witeck Communications, LGBT-inclusive advertising by legacy brands such as these helps make the brand look less stodgy and more relevant to the millennial generation.

TIP!

Traditionally, advertising with coding (such as the use of rainbow flags) and gay-vague ads have been hallmarks of brands marketing to LGBT consumers. Depending on your country, audience's openness to and acceptance of LGBT people, or your industry, the use of symbols or gay vagueness can denote a lack of true openness. Some might say, "Just come out and say it!" Others argue that codes and gay-vague ads strike the right balance.

---

41 | ONLINE AND DIGITAL MARKETING

Online and digital marketing is particularly valuable to the tourism and hospitality industry. These types of marketing offer several notable advantages:

- Online and digital technology can target LGBT customers in specific geographic regions and can reduce advertising production costs. These savings can be used to advertise more or to expand a marketing budget to include more frequency or other channels.

- Trafficking creative is easier with online and digital marketing.
- Every ad is testable.
- Results are measureable.

In many advertising channels, it is difficult to change ads frequently. The opposite is true in the online and digital space. Advertisers can change their ads frequently to see what works best, and they can test creative variants simultaneously with A/B or split testing, which allows marketers to test the effectiveness of varying messages and ads.

Scott Gatz is the founder and CEO of Q.Digital Corporation. A pioneer in digital marketing, he turned his talents exclusively toward the LGBT media space in 2007. His first project was GayCities, a mobile, social, location-based network where people come together to share their favorite experiences in their own towns or around the world. Because of its ease of updating, its cost-effectiveness, advances in mobile and desktop technology, and an overwhelmingly positive consumer response, GayCities is replacing traditional print destination guides.

A trendsetter, Q.Digital is able to cross-pollinate content across sites to provide a focused platform for sponsors and advertisers seeking to reach LGBT audiences. Clients include American Airlines, San Francisco Travel, and Hyatt. Q.Digital's combined properties can provide a complementary or alternative choice to other LGBT media, such as Here Media, which owns *Out*, the *Advocate*, Gay.com, and the Gay Ad Network.

Gatz explains:

Digital is about connecting people to each other and eventually connecting people to brands. This concept has remained the same from the beginning of this industry. It started with messaging boards, then expanded to the creation of the banner ads in 1997, and then into the social media world.

Online is all about creating conversations and creating places to convene and creating interesting and compelling content to converse about. Content is context. In digital, you want to get people talking, and that might mean tweets, reshares, and comments. The game changer is that the Internet is with you wherever you are. It is always on, always with you, with every person, everywhere, all the time.[10]

To illustrate the effectiveness, ease, and value of online advertising, Gatz uses this example: "Let's say you are a hotel and you know that you get most of your customers from three feeder markets. If you choose to advertise in print, you find the biggest papers, negotiate prices, then design, size, resize, and traffic the ad to one or more print publications. Digital has standard formats, and you can buy from one source and end up in many places. With the cost savings compared to print, a hotel can go from focusing on the top three feeder markets to focusing on the top ten feeder markets."[11]

GATZ'S THREE STAGES OF LGBT TRAVEL

Gatz defines the three phases of LGBT travel and how marketers can efficiently use different online and mobile advertising strategies to reach LGBT travelers during each phase.

1. **Inspiration phase.** At this point LGBT travelers are exploring options. They are asking, "Where do I want to go?" Gatz recommends that marketers geographically target their core feeder markets with great content—for example, with advertorials that mix content with a subtle advertising pitch.

2. **Planning phase.** Here the traveler is digging more deeply into a particular destination. This is the time to place (and show) ads that are more specific to the destination. For example, during this phase the local hotel industry has the opportunity to place specific ads for people who are showing interest in visiting a particular destination.

3. **"There" phase.** In the third phase the LGBT visitor is "there"—at the destination—and asking, "What am I doing?" For example, an LGBT traveler may be using the GayCities app, tapping into the Philadelphia page while in Philadelphia. The visitor is probably using a mobile device, and now is the time for mobile ads for events, nightlife, dining, and more.

GATZ'S TIPS FOR ONLINE MARKETING SUCCESS

Gatz offers the following tips for marketing your product, destination, or service online.

1. **The more focused you are, the more successful you will be.** If you were in Times Square and shouted at the top of your lungs, a lot of people would hear you—but would they *listen*? Instead of shouting in Times Square, grab three people who like your offerings and nicely talk about what you have to offer and why it should matter to them. Those three people may become customers. You might have gotten those three customers in Times Square—but it is more likely that you would not have.

2. **Use banner ads.** Set your goals and make your banner ads match them and your target audience. Bad creative banners will kill you. Test three banner ads and see which one performs best. Then use that one.

3. **Make your e-mails stand out.** E-mail can be an effective marketing tool, but inboxes are overloaded. To make your e-mail stand out, you need to be creative.

4. **Use advertorial or branded content.** This strategy can be very effective, but you need to work with an LGBT media outlet and a writer knowledgeable about LGBT travelers to make sure that the content resonates with the audience.

5. **Make your video fit your brand.** Make sure your videos speak to their audience and let the content creators create beautiful content that fits the brand. If you hire an LGBT online influencer or blogger like Davey Wavey, a global YouTube personality and fitness guru, trust him. He knows how to entertain and spark conversation with his online videos.

6. **Take the extra step to talk to the LGBT market with your creative.** If you want to stand out, you have go for it! Make your creative look and sound like you are talking to the LGBT market. Every time a brand does that, the brand wins.

7. **Have a 360-degree marketing outreach strategy.** In addition to advertising, develop PR, communications, online, and other marketing strategies.

MEASURING THE EFFECTIVENESS OF DIGITAL MARKETING

How do you measure the effectiveness of digital marketing? Gatz suggests that you start by creating campaign goals. Only then will you be able to measure their effectiveness. Typical goals include the following:

- **Brand awareness.** Increased brand awareness should happen during the inspiration phase. Look to measures to identify if you are running a successful branding campaign. A brand lift is harder to measure. (*Brand lift* is a positive increase in awareness and perception of a brand as a result of an advertising campaign.)

- **Direct response.** Typically, direct response occurs during the planning phase, when marketers are looking at purchase intent or actual purchases. Use analytics to track referring websites and the purchase percentage. Use tracking codes to help marketers understand the sources of new orders, subscriptions, or other consumer actions.

TIP!

Scott Gatz of Q.Digital offers this word of caution: don't focus solely on direct sales. The metrics are different in the LGBT market. LGBT magazines will not have the same click-through rate as Kayak. The same is true for advertising in mainstream magazines like *Travel and Leisure*. A branding ad in a mainstream magazine will not have the same result as a direct-response ad placement.*

* Interview with Scott Gatz, November 2015.

REACHING THE LGBT MARKET THROUGH GAY AND MAINSTREAM DIGITAL NETWORKS

4 J

Digital is a cost-effective buy because digital networks have done such a good job of identifying the LGBT audience. Digital networks identify the LGBT audience by using demographic, behavioral, purchase-intent, and social targeting algorithms. They collect audience targets across an array of media outlets ranging from niche LGBT websites to premium mainstream websites and mobile apps.

The most relevant LGBT ads are delivered to individual consumers on the basis of specific engagement metrics, interests, and behaviors. Data-driven marketing services make it possible for advertisers to target LGBT people and not just gay media, gay content, and gay-related searches. Gay men, lesbians, and LGBT parents don't just consume gay media; they also visit the *New York Times* website, look at YouTube, and post on Facebook.

In the United States a leading gay media network is the Gay Ad Network, which provides online, mobile, and video advertising services to global and national brands targeting the gay and lesbian community. The Gay Ad Network can reach 25 million global LGBT people on Facebook, provide display ads, and execute a mobile marketing ad campaign from banner ads to text messaging. Here is where the Gay Ad Network excels: it provides LGBT-specific ads in relevant content with relevant context to the LGBT person using both gay and nongay digital media channels. The Gay Ad Network reaches LGBT consumers through direct relationships with LGBT publishers, Google DoubleClick, Microsoft Ad Exchange, Yahoo! Right Media, YouTube, Facebook Exchange (FBX), and other networks. Mark Elderkin, CEO of the Gay Ad Network, explains, "By combining our proprietary data with third-party data and the distribution power of demand-side platforms and ad exchanges, we are able to offer national advertisers a more efficient way to reach their ideal gay consumer targets."[12]

Many companies in the travel industry have turned to the Gay Ad Network to reach LGBT travelers, including American Airlines, Orbitz, MGM Resorts, Switzerland Tourism, Visit Las Vegas, and Amtrak. Each of these advertisers layered an LGBT micro-campaign into their mainstream campaign.

4 J | MARKETING THROUGH MOBILE PHONE APPS

Broadly defined, *mobile marketing* includes advertising, apps, messaging, m-commerce (mobile commerce), and customer relationship management (CRM) on all mobile devices, including smart phones and tablets. The mobile marketing channel allows marketers to foster two-way conversations, customization, personalization, interactivity, and active participation. According to the Mobile Marketing Association's (MMA) "2015 Global Smarties Trends Report," today's mobile marketers focus on deepening human relationships with purpose-driven strategies rooted in human need.

Mobile marketers can learn a lot from effective app-based LGBT tourism marketing, which focuses on connecting, respecting, and talking with LGBT consumers. Grindr and SCRUFF are two apps used by millions of gay men worldwide. Senior Research Director David Paisley from Community Marketing & Insights (CMI) says, "Advertising on Grindr and SCRUFF is actually working well for some folks in the tourism industry who are willing to go there." Paisley's conclusion is supported by CMI research, which shows that interest in travel for nightlife and parties is driven by men. Romance travel is driven by women. According to CMI, when male couples are talking about traveling together, *romance* is not a word that they use a lot. Rather, their focus is on fun and experience.

GRINDR AS A MARKETING CHANNEL

Ad networks and exchanges are valuable for reach, but they can serve up ads that are not relevant to the LGBT consumer. In contrast, smart, targeted advertising on mobile apps like Grindr can enhance the experience for end users by presenting them with travel ideas. "No other paid media have worked as well as mobile apps in reaching certain demographics," says Steve Levin, head of global sales for Grindr. "Travel can be a primary category for low-hanging advertising opportunities and results are strong."[13]

Grindr has over two million daily active users in 192 countries. It launches the app about eight times a day, using an average 2.5 hours a day. Major brands like Live Nation, Visit London, Hyatt, Las Vegas, Uber, Expedia, and hotels.com are advertising with Grindr.

Some advertisers and media buying agencies object to advertising on Grindr. The typical objection is: "It's a hookup app, and we don't want our brand associated with a hookup app." This is an old argument; for a long time advertisers didn't want to advertise in LGBT newspapers because of the salacious ads in the back of the publications. This is a misplaced objection when it comes to the LGBT market, especially gay men. Consider it this way: if your customers are comfortable in Grindr and they are seeing your ad and responding to it, why should you consider Grindr "inappropriate"? Nonetheless, some companies have chosen to work with a media company like *ManAboutWorld* to create a guide that can be advertised on Grindr or SCRUFF so that the company can remain one step removed from the app.

Levin believes that the evolution and increasing public acceptance of mobile dating apps are making advertisers more comfortable with them. It used to be that some members of the gay community would have a Grindr account but not talk much (or at all) about it. Now we see people in bars openly checking their Grindr app. Grindr helps gay men find friends, partners, and husbands. Grindr, like SCRUFF, is also a travel app that helps visitors figure out what to do and where to go. Grindr users

CREATING AN EFFECTIVE MOBILE APP CAMPAIGN

Steve Levin of Grindr offers the following tips for an effective mobile app campaign:

1. Apply creative that is relevant to a very specific audience.
2. Keep the creative fresh and switch it out.
3. Use animated GIFs and video.
4. Mobile advertising is still advertising. It needs consistency.
5. Manage your expectations. Mobile is not a magic wand. You need to manage your expectations for the campaign and keep them realistic.

are not only making appointments for cosmetic surgery as a result of seeing ads on Grindr, they are also buying $5,000 cruises they saw advertised on the app.

Advertisers are used to buying through automated systems and buying programmatically at the best possible price. Allocating dollars to a direct campaign can guarantee results and definite placement. In fact, the response to a direct campaign can be extraordinary. With mobile banner ads purchased through exchanges, advertisers can expect a .1, .2, or .3 response as an industry standard. Direct campaigns can result in a 2–20 percent click-through rate. Advertisers can use these direct campaigns to build up a database or add friends to a Facebook page.

In addition to building a database, other benefits of mobile app advertising are analytics, the ability to geographically target within less than a mile of your business, lower costs for creative, the ability to change creative easily, and the ability to target users by age range.

CASE STUDY

MADONNA AND GRINDR: SELLING TICKETS THROUGH MOBILE

Live Nation, the world's largest live entertainment company, partnered with Facebook's Atlas and Grindr to promote and analyze sales for Madonna's 2015–2016 "Rebel Heart" tour. Grindr launched the Madonna "Rebel Heart" Valentine's Day sweepstakes and advertising campaign for Live Nation. Grindr asked users to (1) change their profile pictures to match Madonna's album cover for a chance to win a chat with the Material Girl herself, and (2) go to Madonna.com to purchase presale tickets for her concert tour launching later that year. The campaign launched one month before her new album, *Rebel*

Heart, was released. The goals were to sell tickets to the upcoming concert tour and to reconnect with her gay fans.[*]

In a joint statement, Facebook and Live Nation said, "The consumer shift to mobile and cross-device engagement has completely upended decades of accepted wisdom about our audiences—not only who they are and how best to reach them but the ways in which various media messages can influence an individual's decision to purchase or ignore."[†]

A post-campaign analysis revealed that by using Atlas, Live Nation was able to tie a whopping 66 percent increase in ticket purchases back to mobile. The increase was attributable to conversions that would otherwise have slipped through the cracks by measuring cookies alone. Because of Atlas's targeting and measurement capabilities, Live Nation was able not only to reach the right audience on the right device at the right time, but also to accurately measure the end result to inform future campaigns.

Grindr—a 100 percent mobile environment with no non-app component—ultimately finished as one of the campaign's top-performing channels. If Live Nation had served Grindr ads using a standard third-party platform, the final analysis would have reported zero tickets sold, and Live Nation would have had no way to gauge the campaign's success. "Moving away from a cookie-based solution is a critical part of improving accuracy, buying more efficiently, driving better performance, and in general having better vision into where your dollars are going as an advertiser," says Adam Kasper, chief media officer at Havas Media North America.

[*] Grindr presentation, LGBT Week, New York, April 2015.
[†] Garrett Sloane, "How Facebook Showed Live Nation That Grindr Ads Sell Madonna Tickets," *Ad Week,* June 25, 2015, www.adweek.com/news/technology/how-facebook-showed-live-nation-grindr-ads-sell-madonna-tickets-165582.

MOBILE MARKETING THROUGH SCRUFF

In 2010 three friends—Johnny Skandros, Eric Silverberg, and Jason Marchant—launched a social networking application called SCRUFF. By 2015 eight million gay men worldwide had begun using the app. Where else can you find eight million self-identified gay men all in one app? It is easy to dismiss SCRUFF as a hookup app, but that judgment misses the marketing opportunity to reach a self-identified gay man who can be targeted within feet of his location and served a highly tailored marketing message via a device that is right in his pocket or even in his hand.

SCRUFF's tagline is "Gay Guys Worldwide." Its mission is to connect gay guys to one another and to the global gay community. SCRUFF was the first iPhone and Android app that allowed gay men to connect on a global scale. Its free version is supported by advertisers, mostly banner ads, and its paid-membership version includes targeted ad campaigns.

"Being global is only possible because of the App Store," says Eric Silverberg. "In the early days of the web, local companies and local brands emerged in different verticals segmented by geography." The app era signaled a shift in consumer behavior, as did mobile phones. "Now, the App Store takes your app and makes it globally discoverable right out of the gate. That was unique. Google is successful globally, but you also have separate search engines and separate indexes."

Silverberg points out that travel has been a core use of SCRUFF. He says that gay men use SCRUFF "to meet local people when they arrive in town to get advice, to hook up, to make friends in a city on an event weekend. It was very early on that people started describing how they were using SCRUFF while they travel."

Silverberg tells the story of a friend who went on a whirlwind global trip. He was in India, Cambodia, Jordan, and Great Britain. He used SCRUFF—especially for Jordan and Cambodia—before he even arrived. He found guys to talk to on SCRUFF, so when he landed he had someone ready to meet him and take him around. He went to gay bars and to house parties, and he took a tour of the Jordanian desert with a new friend for four days.

Because so many gay men are travelers, it is no surprise that in fall 2015 SCRUFF launched *SCRUFF Venture,* a groundbreaking feature that redefined the "hookup" app space and helped distinguish SCRUFF from Grindr, Tinder, Daddyhunt, and other apps. According to SCRUFF, "Unlike most straight travelers, gay guys befriend one another quickly and are comfortable sightseeing and spending the day with fellow travelers they have just met." So SCRUFF set out to create a connection for gay men who travel. In the first week, 20,000 trips were created and dozens of premier events listed. Hundreds of Airbnb listings and dozens of destinations are featured, and the numbers keep rising.[14]

The travel features of *SCRUFF Venture* are an opportunity for travelers and travel suppliers. Specifically:

- "Visiting Now & Arriving Soon" lists guys who are currently traveling in a city or will be visiting a city in upcoming weeks, making them prime targets for marketing messages from hotels, restaurants, and attractions.
- "Ambassadors" are city residents who have pledged to provide friendly advice and recommendations to visitors. Ambassadors offer tour providers a good opportunity to promote local tours.
- Airbnb Integration is used by SCRUFF members with listings on Airbnb and VRBO (Vacation Rentals by Owners). Using Airbnb Integration, marketers can connect travel planning and accommodation booking to generate revenue.

- Local event listings highlight events that allow producers and organizations to more effectively reach travelers and increase visitor attendance.

SCRUFF recognizes that not all travel destinations are safe. "SCRUFF wants to keeping our members safe when they travel, and we can do that with a technical approach to obscure a member's location when in a region with unique risks," says Silverberg. In 2015 SCRUFF launched Gay Travel Advisories, a comprehensive resource dedicated to documenting laws that criminalize same-sex acts across the world. SCRUFF members who travel to one of the nearly ninety countries listed are alerted via an in-app notification of the consequences of conviction under these laws. SCRUFF Gay Travel Advisories was built in partnership with the International Lesbian, Gay, Bisexual, Trans, and Intersex Association (www.ilga.org), the world federation of national and local organizations dedicated to achieving equal rights for lesbian, gay, bisexual, trans, and intersex people. "Some countries have fines, others prison terms, and others the death penalty. We see Gay Travel Advisories as a public service," Silverberg explains.

SCRUFF Benevolads gives free, geographically targeted advertising to selected nonprofit organizations that work within the gay community. Using the Benevolads self-service tool, organizations can easily create and publish ads and then track reach and engagement statistics. Benevolads enables nonprofit organizations to recruit members for sports leagues, promote events, inform SCRUFF members about local health services, and encourage charitable giving in numerous areas.

4K | TEN TIPS TO KEEP YOUR LGBT CAMPAIGN AND YOUR DESTINATION COMPETITIVE

Meryl Levitz, president and CEO of Visit Philadelphia, offers the following tips for keeping your LGBT campaign and destination competitive.

1. **Keep your marketing campaign fresh because nothing stands still.** The consumer, the competition, and the technology will change. Inherent in the travel industry is the need for novelty. The challenges are to adhere to your brand and build out a brand that gives people something new.

2. **The proliferation of more destinations means that you have to identify your brand and your brand promise ever more stringently.** With more destinations to choose from, there will be more clutter. There will also be a need for more funding and the need to market differently to differentiate your destination or product. You have to show that it is worth the trip.

3. **Gay = cool is still true.** Early on, LGBT marketing was seen as edgy, even daring. It still is. As LGBT travel becomes more mainstream, however, you have to ask if your LGBT campaign rings the same kind of bell that it used to—or what you have to do so that you don't lose that edge of being trendy in a good way. "Trendy in a good way" means that everybody else will want to do it.

4. **To be successful, you must ensure a strong foundation.** As stakeholders change, it is important to constantly engage with new stakeholders while continuing to engage with current stakeholders.

5. **High-tech and high-touch are key mantras.** Over time, things change. Philadelphia once banked on an event-based marketing strategy. The strategy then evolved into a social media strategy because social is word of mouth and makes that personal connection. That said, as the world becomes more "high tech," it is important to remain "high touch." The higher tech we get, the higher touch marketers need to be. Being heavy on social media and being heavy with in-person marketing are not mutually exclusive. Rather, they balance and reinforce each other.

6. **Live, work, and play.** People who visit a location and feel welcome there may want to relocate there permanently or open a business there. Longwoods International presented a new study in 2015 titled "Destination Marketing and Economic Development: Creating a Singular Place Brand." That study showed that cities, states, and destinations should use their tourism marketing campaigns as their economic development campaigns. This suggestion is particularly applicable to the LGBT market because there is so much possibility, especially when children are not involved, for LGBT visitors to think about living, working, or opening a business in a place where they feel welcome.

7. **Think differently.** Marketing has to identify the opportunities in the market and figure out how to tie them to the brand and product. Ultimately, you want to build a business with paying customers. The LGBT markets have proved themselves to be early adopters across the board. Levitz provides an example: "Let's say two airlines merged, and both had different global alliances, as was the case with American Airlines and US Airways in 2015. One of the first markets I would go after would be LGBT. What other group has more passports than everyone else? Who is able to take advantage of a travel deal faster? Who else is savvier about miles and affinity cards?" In short: if you are looking to solidify a new business opportunity and gain new customers and build loyalty, explore the LGBT market.

8. **Good marketing has consistent truths.** How you execute your marketing campaign will change over time. Give customers enough information about you and they will self-select. Then the marketer has to realize that the customer has self-selected. If the product is right for him, it is right. If not, it's not. Don't overthink.

9. **Know your customer.** It is not enough to say that your market is the monolithic LGBT, millennial, boomer, or Gen-X market. There are differences between older boomers and younger boomers. Millennial and LGBT markets are multicultural, including people of Asian, African, Latino, and European ethnicities.

10. **Content in context is king.** Content in context means that online ad buying must change. Content creates a specific online experience for the consumer. When the online person is served an ad, he or she wants relevance. Advertising must have a deeper relationship within the context and the content. Placement becomes very important.

4L | THE TEN CLASSIC PRINCIPLES OF SUCCESSFUL LGBT MARKETING

Trends are always evolving, but the baseline for success in LGBT marketing never changes.

1. **Partner with the local LGBT community and the LGBT chamber of commerce.**

2. **Invest money.** The reality is that your competitors are investing in the LGBT market. You should, too.

3. **Appoint strong leadership.** Having a strong leader who sees potential and is willing to ride out any storms is an important factor in the success of LGBT marketing efforts.

4. **Do your research.** The industry standard is to conduct research before the launch of a campaign and to assess results at the one-year, three-year, and five-year marks.

5. **Identify your LGBT appeal.** Not sure if your travel product or destination has LGBT appeal? Find a group of LGBT travelers who've experienced your product and a group who haven't. Ask questions. What did your focus group turn up, good and bad? Simply by talking to customers, marketers can usually find three or four messages that will resonate with the LGBT customer and non-customer.

6. **Talk about it.** Create a dialogue about the LGBT market, or offer training to your staff. Consider a webinar or bring in speakers so that everyone is on the same page.

7. **Never forget safety.** Because the LGBT community has a history of being physically and verbally abused (and worse), travel safety is always a concern, especially for lesbians and trans travelers. If your destination has a problem, such as a major gay bashing, don't ignore it. Jump on it. Show a community-centered response. Your safety reputation affects every area of your business.

8. **Gay men like cities.** Gay men tend to be urban and are more likely to travel to big cities. Men like to meet the locals, and there is often a sexual component to their travel in terms of hooking up with other like-minded gay men in destinations they visit—a reality that we in the travel industry don't talk about much.

9. **Lesbians like the outdoors.** Lesbians tend to do more outdoor, active adventures than gay men do. Stereotypes might suggest that lesbians are budget travelers, but perhaps they just are smarter spenders.

10. **A good reputation is necessary but not sufficient.** Your reputation is an important factor in an LGBT traveler's decision, but you must also present a practical message about why the LGBT consumer should choose your product or service over another.

DISCUSSION QUESTIONS

1. What are some of the pitfalls of not having dedicated marketing efforts and people for the LGBT segment of the travel market? How can you and your organization avoid these pitfalls?

2. Eight touch points are reviewed as strategies for building an effective LGBT marketing campaign. Which of these are the most important to your business or organization? Why?

3. What effect has the changing landscape of LGBT publications had on the way that LGBT travelers get their information?

4. Hosting an LGBT press trip is an important aspect of a successful marketing campaign. In what ways can your organization host an effective LGBT press trip?

5. Looking at Gatz's three stages of LGBT travel, which phases can your campaign execute properly? How?

6. How have apps like Grindr and SCRUFF evolved from hookup apps to become compelling marketing channels?

7. How many of the principles of LGBT marketing listed in this chapter can be implemented in your organization? Explain how you would implement these principles.

4L

5

THE GLOBAL VIEW:
OPPORTUNITIES AND CHALLENGES

CHAPTER SUMMARY

This chapter includes the following sections on domestic and international LGBT destinations and opportunities: Asia; Argentina; Brazil; Canada; China; Colombia; Europe; India; Israel; Japan; Mexico; United Kingdom; and the United States beyond New York and San Francisco.

KEY TERMS

LGBT tourism marketing
gay-friendly destinations
LGBT-friendly city
international LGBT marketing
National Gay and Lesbian Chamber of Commerce (NGLCC)
LGBT chamber of commerce
China Pink-Market Conference
quick response codes
emerging destinations
ITB Berlin
WTM (World Travel Market)
high-tech and high-touch marketing

Guaracino, Jeff, and Salvato, Ed, *Handbook of LGBT Tourism and Hospitality*
dx.doi.org/10.17312/harringtonparkpress/2017.03.hlgbtth.005
© 2017 by Jeff Guaracino and Ed Salvato

LGBT tourism and hospitality are not a one-size-fits-all industry. Different markets are at different spots in the arc of LGBT tourism marketing; some are in their infancy, whereas others are quite advanced. Around the world, laws, politics, religion, customs, history, economics, and education are just a few of the many factors that influence LGBT tourism and hospitality. For this chapter we interviewed numerous LGBT experts and ambassadors from Asia, South and Central America, North America, and Europe. We are grateful to all of them for sharing their approaches and perspectives on the LGBT market in their part of the world.

5A | ASIA:
THE MOST GAY-FRIENDLY DESTINATIONS

Robert Sharp, cofounder, Out Adventures, Toronto, Canada

"The most welcoming of the Asian countries when it comes to LGBT travelers are Thailand, Cambodia, and Japan. Singapore, too. Nothing official—there is a bit of a gay life, probably because of a large percentage of expats working in the financial industries. Note, however, that this doesn't mean they are all doing LGBT-specific outreach. Rather, because of their culture and traditions, they are simply very welcoming to all visitors, including LGBT travelers. For example, Japan has such a polite culture. It's not overly gay welcoming, just polite to everyone. The exception is the Thailand Authority Tourism of New York. Thailand advertises in the LGBT media, conducts press trips, and creates in-person events, among other marketing activities (see Figure 20). Efforts are led mostly by tour operators or other travel suppliers, such as the Granvia Hotel Kyoto in Japan (see section 5J).

"For the future, take note of Myanmar (Burma). With the successful election of the National League of Democracy party at the end of 2015, human rights may evolve and it could become more overtly welcoming to gay travelers.

"No matter where you go in Asia, the higher-end your experience, the more welcome you'll feel. Staff is typically better trained at the high-end venues."

5 B | ARGENTINA:
FIVE TIPS FOR YOUR LGBT BUSINESS

Alfredo H. C. Ferreyra, Buegay Argentina, and Latin America Gay Travel director, Buenos Aires

"We focus in on LGB tourism groups, personalized tourism services, customized tours in Argentina and Latin America, and world-class concierge services. The challenge we face marketing our product and services to LGBT consumers is the financial and economic crisis Argentina is facing in 2016. We don't face interruption in providing LGBT services to consumers or travelers. We don't face the cultural, religious, or societal challenges either. Argentina is well known as a leading country for LGBT rights, including same-sex marriage, identity-change laws (for transgender persons), and civil rights.

"We subscribe to these top-five tips for our business: (1) honesty; (2) a permanent focus; (3) flexibility to adapt our business in a changing marketplace; (4) keeping up with the latest technology; and (5) randomly testing the product we sell to ensure quality."

5 C | BRAZIL:
A STRONG LGBT TOURISM MARKET

Clóvis Casemiro, Double C Turismo, IGLTA board member (1998–2002) and IGLTA Brazil ambassador (2009–2012), São Paulo

"The Brazilian LGBT community is diverse, and, as in most other countries, the LGBT community is concentrated in major cities. The gay community has achieved major milestones in terms of laws, such as marriage equality, adoption of children, and boasts more than two hundred nonprofit groups focusing on health, education, safety, and laws aimed at the LGBT public. Another area of growth is the numerous LGBT Prides across the country, from small towns in the interior of the Amazon to cities, including Rio de Janeiro, Salvador, Porto Alegre, and what is considered one of the largest in the world in São Paulo, and many other major Brazilian cities.

"LGBT tourism in Brazil began to develop in 1998 when for the first time IGLTA [the International Gay and Lesbian Tourism Association] held an LGBT travel-related symposium in Rio de Janeiro. It attracted more than 150 attendees from several countries. After Rio, LGBT tourism developed in São Paulo for Brazilians and foreigners alike.

"What followed in São Paulo was media trips and travel agent familiarization tours from various countries. Today São Paulo is one of the strongest gay destinations in Latin America. The next area of the country to reach out to LGBT travelers was the northeast of Brazil, in cities like Salvador and Recife—each of which enjoys the influence of Europeans who have lived there for many years. Today the two cities are strong representatives of new LGBT destinations.

"With the strength of its tourism sector (hotels, tourist offices, restaurants, receptives—companies that handle the logistics for individuals or groups coming into a destination), Santa Catarina brought to Brazil the first IGLTA convention to take place in South America in 2012 in the beautiful city of Florianópolis. This was in large part thanks to the efforts of Marta Dalla Chiesa, IGLTA board member at the time, owner of Brazil Ecojourneys, and president of ABRAT [the Brazilian gay tourism association]. Because of this, today Florianópolis is one of the most visited Brazilian gay destinations by both locals and foreigners.

"There are two EXPO LGBT events in São Paulo, bringing companies in other industries and tourism to discuss employees and LGBT consumers. We have the support of the NGLCC [National Gay and Lesbian Chamber of Commerce] and LGBT Chamber of Commerce in Argentina. We have the support of the government, through the Ministry of Tourism and EMBRATUR [Brazil's official travel agency, sometimes called the Brazilian Tourist Board], which considers the LGBT tourism segment as a priority in their plans. We do not have agencies that are 100 percent focused on this segment. The majority of travel agencies are gay-friendly and meet all requirements."

Brazil includes LGBT families in its celebration of National Family Day (see Figure 21).

5D | CANADA:
NEW WAYS OF MARKETING
USING CONTENT IN CONTEXT

Tanya Churchmuch, former assistant director, International Media Relations and Leisure Markets, Tourism Montreal

Montreal, Quebec, was one the earliest destinations to begin marketing to LGBT travelers. The effort began in 1996 with a $125,000 campaign. Since then, Montreal has invested more than $2 million to this segment.[1] Today the city focuses on engaging younger travelers because once travelers are introduced to Montreal, they tend to come back again and again. Here are three examples of their most creative marketing campaigns:

- **Montreal Boy: Some Strings Attached** was a six-part web series that aired in 2014. It was developed by the LOGO cable television network in collaboration with Air Canada and Jimmy Lee. The Montreal Boy campaign was tied to LOGO's hit series *RuPaul's Drag Race*. Montreal benefited from editorial content about the city across all LOGO platforms that was supported by a strong social media campaign. To assess return on investment, Montreal measured the number of video views, comments, clicks, actions, and other measures (including media coverage).

- **Do Your Thing in MTL,** a video series hosted by Tourism Montreal's LGBT network QUEER MTL, featured top LGBT entertainers using locations in Montreal as their stage. The premise of the campaign was simple: "No matter who you are or where you come from, Montreal is ready to accept you with open arms." The campaign allowed these celebrities to share their experience in Montreal with fans on their own social networks, encouraging conversations and buzz to build Montreal's LGBT scene. The gay icons included the singer-songwriter Johnny "Gay Pimp" McGovern, comedian DeAnne Smith, Olympic figure skater Johnny Weir, drag queen Mado Lamotte, and trans model Carmen Carrera.

- **Queer of the Year** was a social media campaign built on Facebook and extended to Twitter and YouTube. *Queer* is a term that is not generally recommended for use in marketing, but research shows that younger people often identify with the word. Given Montreal's goal of attracting a younger LGBT demographic, the city thought that using the word was authentic, and it turned out to be the right word for the campaign. Here is how Montreal describes its annual Queer of the Year contest:

> There are a lot of fabulous queers in the world. Gays, lesbians, bisexuals, and transfolk (and all the beautiful identities in between) are spending their leisure time making the world a better place: helping community organizations fundraise, lobbying for equal rights against antiquated legislation or simply being funny and positive individuals. Why not throw a massive, viral internet party and celebrate them?
>
> The "Queer of the Year" contest has arrived. It's equal parts "YouTube reality jovial-ness" and "genuine campaign to salute awesome queers." And it's pretty easy to enter. You submit a short video that attests to why you might be the "Queer of the Year."[2]

5E | CHINA: A MARKET OPPORTUNITY

Community Marketing & Insights forged a partnership with the organization Shanghai LGBT Professionals and twenty LGBT corporate partners across China to help companies explore the market opportunities in the Chinese LGBT community. The initial study—released in 2014 at the first-ever China Pink-Market Conference—reported results from 8,000 survey respondents. That study found the following:

- Those who are more "out" and involved in China's emerging LGBT community tend to be young adults. Companies reaching out to China's LGBT community should therefore use imagery, language, and media that appeal to a young-adult demographic.

- More Chinese men than women responded to the survey, but lesbians and bisexual women indicated that they are far more likely to be out to friends, family, and colleagues and far less likely to indicate that they were completely closeted. Both the male and female markets represent significant opportunity.

- Because of the absence of legal protection for LGBT people both in life and in the workplace, LGBT-related policies are a big concern for LGBT people in China. When marketing to LGBT people there, companies should demonstrate support for policy-related causes and communicate that support through LGBT organizations, events, and especially mainstream media when possible.

- Eighty percent of respondents indicated that pressure from their families is their biggest concern, especially for young students (85 percent). Family plays a very important role in the lives of Chinese LGBT people. Companies that convey a message about family support for LGBT people can create an important emotional bond with LGBT consumers.

- Young LGBT people in China are mobile-obsessed. Because most Chinese LGBT people are communicating via mobile devices, companies reaching out to them should be sure that the mobile experience is welcoming. "Welcome signals" may include same-sex-couple imagery in mobile-optimized websites and apps, as well as gender-neutral terminology.

- Instant messaging and social media have become the largest personal communication tools for Chinese LGBT people: 95 percent and 81 percent of respondents, respectively, rated WeChat and Weibo as the top social media platforms they use, making these two the leaders among non-LGBT-specific social media sites. Students between eighteen and twenty-one have more interaction with Weibo, whereas survey respondents twenty-five and above are more likely to interact with Wechat. Companies should increase social media marketing when reaching out to young Chinese LGBT people and make sure that their content is LGBT-inclusive and supportive.

- Quick response (QR) codes, deal sites, and social media reviews draw the most weekly ad interactions. The research points to a gender gap in preferred media. Chinese gay and bisexual men engage more with LGBT apps (45 percent) and LGBT websites/blogs (44 percent), while Chinese lesbians and bisexual women interact more with network and cable TV (42 percent) and online streaming video (42 percent).

- Chinese lesbians and bisexual women travel more than gay and bisexual men, both domestically and internationally: 68 percent of lesbians and bisexual women and 53 percent of gay and bisexual men had taken at least one domestic leisure trip or vacation in the preceding twelve months.

- The top five domestic destinations for Chinese LGBT people are Beijing, Shanghai, Hangzhou, Chengdu, and Xiamen. For decades, travel has been a huge part of the international LGBT economy, and this appears to be true in China as well.

- Forty-nine percent of Chinese lesbians and bisexual women and 34 percent of Chinese gay and bisexual men indicated that they have a current passport, and this number goes up to 54 percent for Chinese LGBT people ages twenty-five and above.

- In the preceding year, 30 percent of Chinese lesbians and bisexual women and 18 percent of Chinese gay and bisexual men had taken at least one leisure trip or vacation in a foreign country or Hong Kong, Macau, or Taiwan. Other popular Asian destinations included Thailand, South Korea, Japan, and Malaysia. Visits to the United States and European countries were also fairly popular among Chinese LGBT people.

- Eighteen percent of Chinese LGBT people indicated that they had traveled to participate in an LGBT community event in the preceding twelve months. Those who travel with same-sex partners or LGBT friends internationally are more likely to attend LGBT events. The most popular LGBT events are circuit party or dance events and Pride.

Rich Campbell, founder of Atlantis Events and RSVP vacations, notes: "China is not gay hostile; it's just not that open. The Chinese gay market is there. The bigger issue in China is time. Most workers get very little holiday time. They get days, not weeks." For this reason, Campbell says, the Chinese market needs five- to seven-day cruises. His cruises are typically ten days. An option is to take a ten-day cruise and split it into two five-day itineraries. Atlantis has chartered four cruises out of Hong Kong and two out of Shanghai and has taken visitors to Vietnam on four different cruises.

5 E

5F | COLOMBIA: FIVE TIPS FROM AN EMERGING DESTINATION

Felipe Cardenas, CEO, Colombian LGBT Chamber of Commerce, Bogotá

"I am located in Bogotá, Colombia, an emerging LGBT destination. I run the Colombian LGBT chamber of commerce with an interesting group of members composed of hotels, bars, clubs, coffee shops, restaurants, and tourist venues in Bogotá and in Cartagena. We promote different packages for amazing LGBT travel experiences here through travel agencies such as the Gallery Travel, GayTravel, Kiboko Travel, Viajes Chapinero, and Carreño Tours. For example, the LGBT Halloween Circuit in Bogotá is a five-day event with parties. In 2014, 8,000 foreign LGBT visitors came for this festival.

"The challenge we face is mapping the right demand affected by the right promotion. Bilingual advertisement was blocked until 2013. There are also lingering misperceptions and mindsets about safety and visiting Colombia. To overcome these challenges, we have been pushing a strong online marketing effort combined with physical promotion abroad by personally attending different events, meeting potential visitors face-to-face. We want to show real data and facts about how LGBT tourism is booming in this country. This combination is getting the right results.

"Even though Colombian society is deeply Catholic and conservative, cities such as Bogotá and Cartagena have become so cosmopolitan that it is not that hard finding suppliers and vendors for LGBT tourism experiences. The message of economic prosperity with an emerging segment such as the LGBT one is not bothering anyone in the tourism industry here.

"My top five tips for other emerging destinations would be: (1) offer real data; (2) showcase success cases from countries or destinations you look up to; (3) correctly state what you offer so as not to create false expectations; (4) partner with key organizations at home and abroad to present your destination; and (5) create a strong internal network of reliable suppliers and operators to manufacture the right LGBT travel experience."

5 G | EUROPE: TIPS ON THE LESBIAN MARKET

Betti Keese, owner of GoBeyond Vacations and Leztrek, Germany, Austria, and Switzerland

"I have a small travel agency for the lesbian community, offering tailor-made tours mostly for individual travelers. I also offer consulting on lesbian travel to hotels, destinations, and other travel-related businesses. Reaching the LGBT market, especially the lesbian market, has always been challenging. Lesbian consumers are especially hard to reach, as they often are not part of the 'scene' and do not access the relevant media or websites. Creating the right offers for a part of the LGBTI community that tends to be slightly less visible has been a lot of trial and error. There are no relevant studies about this specific market, so I conducted my own study on the German lesbian travel market to get insight. I try to keep up with all relevant media, blogs, and websites from around the globe, too. I always make sure the hotels and other accommodations know who my guests are so that they feel welcome right from the start."

5 H | INDIA: CULTURAL, RELIGIOUS, AND SOCIETAL CHALLENGES

Rajat Singla, director, Pink Vibgyor

"We are located in New Delhi, India, and offer travel services to the Indian subcontinent ranging from gay group tours and personalized tours from budget to high-end. Our challenge is that India is a reserved society, and reaching a dedicated market is always a hurdle. In India, we do not have 100 percent gay hotels, saunas or spas, restaurants, resorts, or government-licensed guides. We have to market our India tours as gay-friendly and the same goes for the services and the hotels. The market is very price-sensitive and not very loyal to the service provider; a slight change of cost and the clientele shifts from one provider to another without thinking about the quality of the services.

"In India, there are cultural, religious, and societal challenges. Many people with a modern outlook are still closeted and do not want to come out. People understand about equal rights but still do not want to talk about it. Culture and history are very strong. The Western influence is helping people come out and speak up for their rights. India tourism is also not open for promoting India as an LGBT holiday destination. Thus, we have to participate every time in the Gay Pavilion hosted by IGLTA in ITB Berlin and WTM [World Travel Market] London, two of the world's largest consumer and trade travel shows.

"To overcome our challenges we conduct training sessions in budget and luxury Indian hotels on LGBT tourism and its importance to the Indian economy. We participate in many travel shows to promote India as a gay-friendly destination. We do marketing on Facebook and regular mailers to reach potential LGBT travelers. We participate in Pride parades in metropolitan cities of India—for example Delhi, Mumbai, and Bangalore. We try to understand the success of LGBT marketing in the global world and use the right method and try to be innovative in whatever we do."

51 | ISRAEL: MARKETING LGBT TOURS IN TEL AVIV

Russell Lord, Kenes Tours, Tel Aviv, Israel

Tel Aviv has become one of the world's leading LGBT tourist destinations. Perhaps the city most accepting of LGBT people and tourists in the Middle East, the destination's three hundred days of sun a year, beautiful beaches, famous culinary scene, and nightlife appeal to many LGBT visitors. So does the city's central location. Popular sightseeing areas are a short drive from Tel Aviv; visitors can go to the places and see the architecture and art that they have heard about since they were kids: Bethlehem, Masada, the Dead Sea, Jerusalem. (Jerusalem had launched an LGBT tourism campaign in 2007 that was ultimately canceled because of controversy.) Tel Aviv was the first city in Israel to celebrate Pride events, the first official Pride Parade taking place in 1998. GayCities.com ranked Tel Aviv as the World's Best Gay Tourism Destination, and CNN ranked the city, which also hosts a Gay Film Festival, as "one of the 10 best gay honeymoon hotspots."

Tel Aviv Municipality allocates many resources to promote and support the LGBT community. In 2014 the municipality invested more than $600,000 to support the Gay Community Center and Pride Week events. Tel Aviv's Gay Parade is entirely financed by the municipality. With the Ministry of Tourism, the municipality also invests around $250,000 in promoting LGBT tourism in countries like Germany, Italy, the United Kingdom, France, the United States, South America, and (in unofficial marketing) Russia. The average gay tourist stays in Tel Aviv a little more than three nights and spends around $245 a day (including accommodation)—40 percent more than the average tourist. For Pride alone, 30,000 LGBT visitors come to Tel Aviv.[3]

Kenes Tours Global Service Ltd. is Israel's premier tour operator. Russell Lord, tour operator and travel consultant for Kenes, has been leading the way for LGBT tourism in Israel since the 1990s. "Just like blue-haired ladies like to travel together, LGBT travelers want the same thing because it is a common thread along with common humor and common life experiences," says Lord. "On one of our gay tours, the guests raised their glasses to toast Bette Midler on her birthday."

Lord is a gay rights pioneer. He and his partner, Avi, had already been together twenty-three years before they decided to go to Canada to get married. When they returned to Israel, they went to the Israeli Supreme Court to have their marriage recognized. "We didn't do it so we could be together; we were already together. Avi wanted to do this so that when young people get together—either two guys or two girls—they will feel like everyone else. Getting married would be the natural course of events for them, just as they take out a passport or a driver's license. It would say on their ID card that they are married. That sounded cool to me, so why not."

Lord offers insight into the success of Kenes Tours. "At Kenes, we build itineraries for people who want something to be geared to their interest. Israel is a small country. If you are interested in religion, history, or architecture, we can build a program around that." Lord took that business model a step further and started to custom-build tours around group interests, especially for gay travelers who are not in the closet. "Other tour operators were asking for recommendations about gay bars for their customers," Lord says. "So I knew there was a market there."

He continues, "Israel isn't solely a religious destination. Jerusalem is where Judaism, Christianity, and Islam began, but that doesn't make Israel any more religious than any other country. Tel Aviv is a city that was founded in 1909 and has a young, pioneering spirit to it." Here are Lord's tips for success in Israel's LGBT travel market:

1. **Success is all about service.** Gay tourism is similar to upscale straight tourism.

2. **Stop worrying—the Internet is not going to put tour operators out of business.** All businesses need someone who specializes in the LGBT market to connect the dots to make a great LGBT trip happen. The best LGBT tour operators help visitors make the most of their time and spend their money in the right way.

3. **Gear your program to the interests of LGBT visitors.** For example, visitors to Israel like the traditional basic tours, but when they go to the Holocaust Museum they want to hear about the LGBT community in the 1930s and the 1940s. Lord says, "We take our LGBT visitors to the memorial to all the Holocaust victims in front of the gay community center. It is not on your basic tourism map."

4. **Recognize differences in the length of stay.** Tourists from nearby countries or within the region tend to come to Israel for long-weekend party tourism, whereas travelers from North America and other farther away countries tend to avoid the late-night parties or are "party light." Lord summarizes the difference concisely: "They don't want to come all this way to do what they can do closer to home. They are here for the Israel experience."

5J | JAPAN: WELCOMING INTERNATIONAL LGBT GUESTS TO A CONSERVATIVE COUNTRY

Shiho Ikeuchi, director of overseas marketing, Hotel Granvia, Kyoto, Japan

Shiho Ikeuchi is on the forefront of LGBT marketing in Asia. She faces the challenges of marketing a hotel in a socially conservative foreign destination that is not very well known to the LGBT travel segment. "I see a huge potential for LGBT tourism to Japan," says Ikeuchi. "We have a long way to go because Japanese society, which is socially conservative, doesn't yet fully understand LGBT issues. However, LGBT travelers are trendsetters. I am confident that once Japan becomes popular among LGBT travelers, the economic impact will be enormous."

The numbers support Ikeuchi's prediction. LGBT tourism is one of the fastest-growing segments in Japan. The total number of international travelers to Japan in 2014 was 13.41 million, and the total amount they spent was over $20 billion (representing a 43 percent increase over the previous year).[4] Ikeuchi notes, "If you conservatively estimate that 3 percent of the total numbers are LGBT travelers to Japan, that means approximately 402,000 LGBT visitors came to Japan in 2014 and spent approximately U.S. $600 million." Ikeuchi estimates that at least 5,000 LGBT guests stayed at Hotel Granvia in 2014, spending over $1 million, including the hotel rate and other spending at the hotel.

Ikeuchi launched the LGBT travel initiative after an IGLTA convention, announcing a same-sex wedding package. According to Ikeuchi, "That press release about our same-sex wedding package shocked the world; many international media organizations wrote about it. Japanese media soon followed suit, running reports in major newspapers and travel magazines, as well as on TV news."[5]

Japan's gay civil rights movement is gathering momentum. Over 55,000 participants (a record number) took part in a recent Tokyo Rainbow Pride. Several nonprofit Japanese organizations now support marriage equality, and a nonpartisan association of Japan's diverse political parties has joined forces to establish a group dedicated to ending discrimination against sexual minorities. One of the three concepts for the Tokyo Olympics in 2020 is "Accepting one another—Unity in diversity." Ikeuchi believes that this goal will be a very important focus for all Japan and will help frame the argument for LGBT rights.

Although many people think that Japan is too conservative to welcome LGBT travelers, it may be the case that Japan simply hasn't been promoted as an LGBT-friendly destination, and visitors may be surprised to see that LGBT travelers are welcomed at almost every place they visit. Tokyo is the most gay-friendly area in Japan, Shinjuku Nicho-me in particular (a popular gay section of Toyko). Other compelling areas, such as Kyoto, are not quite as familiar to LGBT travelers.

Ikeuchi notes a key difference between Asian LGBT travelers and Western LGBT travelers: because many LGBT people in Japan and other Asian countries are still in the closet, LGBT couples try not to be noticeable as couples to others in public. Destination weddings are a trend in Asia, and many Asian LGBT couples have their weddings outside their country. In contrast, Western LGBT travelers are more open about their sexual orientation. They often notify Ikeuchi's Hotel Granvia of their anniversaries and other special occasions, just as straight couples do.

Ikeuchi offers five tips for marketing to LGBT travelers.

1. **Invest in employee education and training.** Lack of awareness is the biggest obstacle in reaching LGBT travelers. The Hotel Granvia regularly holds study meetings to explore basic LGBT issues for its employees, and an average of seventy staff members have attended each class for the last two years. The goals of the classes are simple: to serve LGBT guests better and to avoid careless remarks.

2. **Be visible as LGBT-friendly.** Ikeuchi believes that it is important to actively demonstrate that her hotel is LGBT-friendly. In addition to taking classes, all the hotel's concierge staff members wear a rainbow pin on their uniform. It was the manager of the concierge team (a straight man) who suggested wearing the pin. It may seem just a small step, but it is an important one.

3. **Direct marketing to the LGBT segment is key.** Ikeuchi usually separates LGBT tourism and general tourism in her marketing efforts. According to Ikeuchi, "LGBT networking is connected strongly within the segment, and once you gain connections, your network starts spreading the word. I have gained relationships with many travel agents, consulting companies, and media that feature LGBT tourism by participating in LGBT-related travel trade shows. Providing the right information to the right market is the key. Obviously, we can't run advertisements for gay male packages in lesbian magazines. It is wise to avoid promoting gay weddings in the countries where same-sex weddings are illegal."

4. **Create LGBT-specific products.** Having a product that features LGBT guests is a key to reaching the market. The Hotel Granvia's same-sex wedding package delivers a clear message that the hotel is gay-friendly. It includes a Buddhist wedding ceremony, traditional Japanese wedding attire for two, seasonal bouquets, limousine service to and from the wedding venue temple, a traditional wedding-night dinner for two, daily breakfast, and a three-night stay in a luxurious Junior Suite room. Ikeuchi notes, "We have had many comments from our guests that they chose the Hotel Granvia Kyoto because they saw the same-sex wedding package that we offer. Even though the guest was not planning to have a wedding, the package attracts LGBT tourists and it provides motivation to the guest for selecting us."

5. **Be trend-conscious.** LGBT travelers are known as trendsetters, and there is a lot to learn from them. Ikeuchi puts it succinctly: "I always try to stay abreast of what is new and attractive, and use that learning in my outreach to LGBT travelers in order to attract them to the hotel."

Masaki Higashida, founder and president of Beyond Tokyo, observes: "We operate a tour company called Beyond Tokyo in Tokyo, Japan, offering innovative and creative walking tours such as 'Sex and the Sushi' to culturally curious travelers. We don't face specific challenges marketing our products and services to LGBT consumers. The LGBT communities represent a broad and dynamic variety of interests and preferences, just like their heterosexual counterparts. Our recent market research shows that there is no remarkable difference between gay and straight travelers visiting Japan in terms of the sites and activities they're interested in. We target all culturally curious and artistically inclined travelers instead of focusing solely on the so-called 'gay market,' yet 30 percent of our customers are LGBT people and their friends.

"A well-defined target market is the first element of our marketing strategy. Though the Japanese take great pride in showing hospitality, most hotels and touring companies are struggling to provide an LGBT-friendly atmosphere because of the lack of LGBT rights awareness. The language barrier exacerbates the communication issues. To overcome, deflect, and minimize these sensitive challenges, we offer various vendors sensitivity training in dealing with LGBT individuals as well as support in marketing strategy. My number-one tip is to do your homework and know your target customers because there is no such thing as 'the gay market' in Japan."

5K | MEXICO: A GAY-FRIENDLY BUT MACHO COUNTRY

Ron Kuijpers, gaytoursmexico by MMT, Cancún

"We operate in Mexico's main tourism spot and offer all services needed by our clients, including transfers, hotel reservations, day excursions, and multiday tours. We specialize in tailor-made tours for LGBT people. The largest challenge we face is reaching customers when they are here; we sell day excursions, but it is hard to reach our target market because they are staying in a huge number of hotels within the region. The challenge for multiday tours is mainly having good and trustworthy partners who are willing to sell us tours. On the hotel reservations, the main problem is not having a specialized booking engine for gay and gay-friendly hotels in Mexico. The mainstream booking engines do little in this segment.

"To overcome these challenges, we are working on setting up our own gay and gay-friendly hotel reservation system. We are promoting our tours in country-specific websites. Eighty percent of Mexico's inbound tourists come from only ten countries. We supplement with social media promoting our tours. As it relates to cultural, religious, and societal challenges, Mexico is generally a gay-friendly but macho country. Same-sex marriage has been legal since 2012, but the Mexican Tourism Board just started in 2015 to promote to the LGBT visitor. There are plenty of gay venues in Mexico, including bars, discos, saunas, hotels, and other hospitality and tourism services. The challenge is to bring them together under one umbrella. We overcome, deflect, or minimize these sensitive challenges by working closely together and doing a lot of market research."

5 L | UNITED KINGDOM: REACHING LGBT TRAVELERS IS ALWAYS A CHALLENGE

Jonathan Mountford, managing director of Made, London

"We offer access to attractions and museums, including the National Gallery, and West End musicals such as *Kinky Boots, Wicked, Sunset Boulevard,* and *Mamma Mia!* Reaching the LGBT market effectively is always a challenge, mostly owing to the absorption of the market into the mainstream. LGBT consumers are becoming harder to pinpoint; therefore, targeting the right section of the market with the right products and services is quite a challenge. We engage heavily with the LGBT community via events such as Pride, not only in London but all around the country, in places such as Brighton and Liverpool. Our strong relationship with the International Gay and Lesbian Tourism Association (IGLTA) is a prime example of how networking events and well-managed partnerships can overcome the challenges of effectively reaching the LGBT market.

"The U.K. is generally very open and accepting to all LGBT tourists, and most publications and organizations treat each service or product on their own merit and with a forward-thinking, open-minded attitude. However, there are certain publications that still retain a religious or 'old-fashioned' moral standard and can prove to be sensitive when advertising an LGBT-targeted product. Similarly, religious-orientated attractions can have trepidation when interacting with the LGBT market. Open discussion, education, and solid factual evidence seem to open doors and relax most opposition to the LGBT travel market."

In addition to the two "gay favorites" in the United States, New York and San Francisco, several other U.S. cities have been extremely successful in marketing to LGBT travelers. Here we offer case studies on two such cities, Fort Lauderdale and Philadelphia.

FORT LAUDERDALE, FLORIDA: TRANSFORMING A DESTINATION THROUGH LGBT TOURISM MARKETING

Nikki Grossman, president, Greater Fort Lauderdale Convention and Visitors Bureau (CVB)

Greater Fort Lauderdale has transformed itself from the college spring-break capital of the United States into a sophisticated destination built on LGBT tourism. A symbol of the city's progress: Fort Lauderdale invented the wet T-shirt contest at a place then called the Candy Store Lounge. Today the lounge is a Ritz Carlton, and Greater Fort Lauderdale is home to the highest concentration of same-sex households in the country—having replaced San Francisco as the LGBT capital of the United States. How did Fort Lauderdale transform itself from a tacky, seedy spring-break location into a major LGBT travel destination? Nikki Grossman recalls:

In 1985, 380,000 college students invaded Fort Lauderdale for spring break. MTV was filming at one end of the beach as young revelers were going wild. On the other end, Philip Morris was handing out free cigarettes and Budweiser was handing out free beer to college students. The destination hoisted a white flag, basically surrendering itself to the college students.

But local businesses did not support the surrender. Hoteliers approached the Greater Fort Lauderdale CVB and said, "If you will help us create a new market, we will make an investment in our properties. We will increase our average daily rate to attract higher-end visitors." The hotel owners asked the CVB to identify an alternative tourism market for Fort Lauderdale to replace the spring-break business. If the CVB could find a replacement, the hoteliers said that they would "stop letting these kids run their business plans."

Catering to a new group of tourists would be a challenge. As Grossman explains, "It is very easy for a destination and the hotels to cater to college students. You do nothing, and you cater to college kids. It is very easy to give student travelers what they want: cheap beer and cheap eats. Give students the cheapest hotel rate and allow the highest number of people to occupy a hotel room. Give them *Girls Gone Wild* and you've satisfied the demand of the college student travel segment."

In determining the direction that its rebranding efforts would take, Fort Lauderdale made a key decision: it wanted to be a warm, welcoming destination to nontraditional markets. It decided to focus its efforts on the African American, LGBT, family-reunion, and other travel segments that the industry itself wasn't doing a good job of reaching. Grossman notes, "At that time, the industry was all about the big leisure travel market. We asked ourselves, how do we get more families? How do we get the higher-end travelers? We looked at the transformational opportunity with a different eye. What kind of traveler was going to be a fit? What and who would fit best on what Greater Fort Lauderdale wanted to become?"

From the beginning, the CVB kept its eye on a key variable: price point. Greater Fort Lauderdale wanted to become a chic but affordable destination. "When you look at Miami to the south or Palm Beach to the north, being affordable was pretty easy," Grossman explains. "We knew what price point we wanted to seek. We didn't want to be a low-rated destination—something that people would consider 'cheap.' We wanted to be an affordable luxury destination. Fortunately, we are graced with optimal geography. We have the beach, the Everglades, adventure, the wild side, and the mild side. The destination itself became a niche, and we found niches in the universe of travelers who were looking for something experiential, a destination that had bragging rights but something still affordable."

The CVB realized that Greater Fort Lauderdale had everything the LGBT travel market was looking for. In fact, all the signs pointed to the LGBT market. Grossman describes LGBT travelers: "They are discerning travelers looking for a luxury product. We all settled on the fact that the LGBT market would be a great place to concentrate our efforts for future growth. We didn't know at that time that the LGBT segment would go beyond leisure to also entail association business (such as the National Gay Pilots Association and the National LGBT Bar Association) and the different associations that would come along with the LGBT business."

Local businesses were quick to provide information about their LGBT customers' wants and needs. "As we were getting started, we had people in our own community who were business owners and hotel owners who were willing to share with us the needs of the LGBT traveler. We didn't have to research the market. We had people who were willing to share with us, help us develop our destination, and market it." The takeaway message here: it takes a village.

Ultimately, it didn't take long for the early naysayers to get on board, as LGBT travelers showed themselves willing to try a visit to Fort Lauderdale. "They were willing to say, 'Wow, there is a place we have never been, and it's called Fort Lauderdale," Grossman says, although some had come for spring break or had spent their early years visiting their grandparents in Fort Lauderdale.

Fort Lauderdale's enormous success as an LGBT travel destination has benefited not only the travelers but also the city and its businesses. "Because adult LGBT trav-

5 M

elers came here and felt very comfortable here, we were able to grow the market and to create a destination product that better reflects what the LGBT travel demands are," Grossman explains. "One of the most positive things that came out of identifying LGBT travelers as a fit for us was that ultimately their travel wants and demands created a far better product for Fort Lauderdale. LGBT travel enhanced Greater Fort Lauderdale as a destination, and it was a gift to us that we were found to be a product that the LGBT market appreciated."

The numbers speak to Fort Lauderdale's success. Since the beginning of the transformation, Fort Lauderdale has seen $1 billion in investment, nearly $500 million of which was private investment in existing properties and a couple of newly built properties. It all started in 1990, when the Harbor Beach Marriott came onto the scene. Today Fort Lauderdale is home to a Four Seasons, a Ritz Carlton, a Conrad, the Atlantic Hotel, a W Hotel, and several B Ocean properties. Enhancements and improvements have also been made to the airport, the port, the roads, and the beaches.

And what of other Florida destinations that market to LGBT travelers, such as Key West (which began its outreach to LGBT travelers before Fort Lauderdale)? Grossman sees mutual benefits to all the destinations: "I feel like there is friendly competition among these communities that gay travelers prefer. We are not necessarily to-the-death competitors. I think there is a synergy."

And what of the future? Grossman vows that it will be "high-tech and high-touch. We are never going to lose the hand-to-hand or the face-to-face connection with the traveler." As an example, Grossman points to a campaign that took place in the winter of 2015: "As part of our marketing campaign, we did remote broadcasts from the beach, talking live to people waiting at a bus stop in cold Chicago. While they were talking to me live from the Fort Lauderdale beach at a highly interactive bus shelter, someone handed them an airline ticket to Greater Fort Lauderdale. It was so important for us to do face-to-face time with that one person or ten people at the bus stop. The high-tech talk from the beach to the bus stop was supported by a PR campaign. We benefited greatly from TV media coverage.

"There is no market that doesn't get our personal attention. I want our meeting planners and corporate customers and leisure visitors to know that we are diverse and culturally friendly, and I want them to know we have a personal interest in them as visitors. We never say, 'We need to put an ad out there.' We always talk about the financial return to the destination and what we want to get out of the ad. It is about money, but also cultural exchange and personal attention. It is not just about the advertising or the marketing. It is about the relationship."

PHILADELPHIA, PENNSYLVANIA:
GET YOUR HISTORY STRAIGHT AND YOUR NIGHTLIFE GAY

Meryl Levitz, president and CEO of Visit Philadelphia

Philadelphia is a global leader in LGBT tourism marketing. In 2003 the Greater Philadelphia Tourism Marketing Corporation (GPTMC) made LGBT travel history, forging a bold new path when it announced an unprecedented three-year, $1 million LGBT marketing campaign called Philadelphia—Get Your History Straight and Your Nightlife Gay. One year later, GPTMC made travel history again by creating the world's first commercial for a destination aimed at gay travelers. The commercial aired on the Comcast Cable Network. GPTMC also partnered with Orbitz to air the thirty-second Pen Pals commercial in key markets around the United States.

According to Mark Segal, publisher of the *Philadelphia Gay News* and author of *And Then I Danced: Traveling the Road to LGBT Equality* (Open Lens, 2015), describes Philadelphia as "America's most LGBT-friendly city," citing a long list of progressive laws enacted well before most other cities enacted similar laws, an effective and inclusive LGBT community relationship with the heterosexual community, and the award-winning and trendsetting John C. Anderson low-income LGBT-friendly senior housing center. The city has scored 100 percent on the Human Rights Campaign's Municipality Equality Index.

Ultimately, tourist businesses need to see results. Between 2003 and 2011, LGBT visitation to Greater Philadelphia was on the rise. The GPMTC (now known as Visit Philadelphia) partnered with Community Marketing & Insights from the very beginning to measure the effect of the campaign. Here are the results over time:

- In 2010 Philadelphia ranked among the top-ten destinations visited by LGBT travelers for the first time. In 2003, when GPTMC first began advertising in this market, Philadelphia did not rank in the top twenty. The momentum of the LGBT travel segment has contributed to overall growth in visitation to Greater Philadelphia.

- Philadelphia is now a top-ten leisure market for gay and lesbian travelers in the eighteen-to-thirty-five age range. The popularity of the destination with young travelers suggests a bright future for the city.

- Gay and lesbian travel to Philadelphia did not slow down during the Great Recession. Though national LGBT travelers reported a slight decrease in travel activity in 2009, LGBT visitors to Philadelphia reported a net increase in their overall travel; 35 percent increased their travel activity and only 23 percent decreased it.

- Gay and lesbian hotel visitors are spending more and staying longer in Philadelphia than they did in 2005, when research was last conducted on Philadelphia's gay and lesbian market. Per-day spending increased 21 percent over five years, from $726 in 2005 to $878 in 2010. Length of stay increased 24 percent, from 2.5 nights in 2005 to 3.1 nights in 2010.

- Awareness of the Philadelphia—Get Your History Straight and Your Nightlife Gay creative and tagline are strong. Of respondents to a Visit Philadelphia survey, 43 percent said they were familiar with at least one of the advertisements shown, GPTMC's iconic Betsy Ross–inspired ad from 2003 still being the most frequently recognized. And 14 percent of respondents were able to correctly write the campaign's tagline without any prompting.

- Those familiar with the campaign are spending more and staying longer in the Philadelphia region. Visitors familiar with the campaign spent an average of $1,013 per party on their stay, 36 percent more than the $743 spent by visitors unfamiliar with the campaign. "Aware" visitors stayed an average of 3.5 nights, compared to 3.0 for those unfamiliar with the campaign. That number climbs to 4.4 nights for visitors who can identify the campaign's tagline.

- Visitors aware of the campaign were more likely to stay in a hotel on their visit (82 percent compared to 63 percent for unaware visitors). They were also more likely to choose luxury or boutique hotels (43 percent compared to 20 percent for unaware visitors).

- Visitors aware of the campaign were less motivated by free offerings when choosing a hotel stay (such as free Internet access, breakfast, and parking). Instead, they were more interested in factors like a hotel's brand reputation and outreach and its proximity to gay bars and restaurants.

- Many gay and lesbian visitors show equal or greater interest in vacation activities that are not LGBT-specific. When asked their reasons for visiting Philadelphia, top responses include "been there before and liked it," "visit friends and family," and "see local historic sites."

- More gay and lesbian visitors said that their reason for visiting Philadelphia was a nongay event (29 percent) than an LGBT event (24 percent).

- Philadelphia's gay and lesbian hotel visitors are extremely loyal; 90 percent reported that they had visited before, and 84 percent intended to return within the next year. And 38 percent consider themselves to be frequent visitors. Because of their familiarity with the city, these visitors are able to explore different aspects of the region each time they return.

- Gay and lesbian hotel visitors are spending 57 percent more per travel party than general-market visitors—$878 compared to $559. Hotels are the primary beneficiary, as lodging spending has risen 75 percent, but gay and lesbian visitors also spend more than average in Philadelphia's restaurants (68 percent more on food and beverages) and stores (52 percent more on shopping).[6]

DISCUSSION QUESTIONS

1. Explain why the Chinese LGBT community offers an important business opportunity.
2. This chapter explores several examples to illustrate the global perspectives on LGBT tourism and hospitality efforts. Which ones are relevant to you? Why?

6

TRENDS AND
INDUSTRY RESOURCES

CHAPTER SUMMARY

This part offers a wealth of
resources for those in the
hospitality and tourism
business—market research:
companies, data, surveys,
and reports; associations
and conventions; advocacy
organizations; conferences
and expositions; further
reading; and an annotated
bibliography.

KEY TERMS

market research
Community Marketing &
    Insights (CMI)
LGBT marketing
LGBT conferences
LGBT travel organizations
LGBT academic travel research
event tourism
gay tourist motivation
gay tourism
gay-friendly travel
gay space
gay-parented family tourism

Guaracino, Jeff, and Salvato, Ed, *Handbook of LGBT Tourism and Hospitality*
dx.doi.org/10.17312/harringtonparkpress/2017.03.hlgbtth.006
© 2017 by Jeff Guaracino and Ed Salvato

LGBT industry conferences, advocacy organizations, business associations, chambers of commerce, and human rights organizations can provide additional educational, sales, networking, and marketing opportunities for those interested in the LGBT tourism and hospitality industry. This chapter provides information about some of the most important organizations and conferences. Increasingly, there are market-specific resources and associations that specialize in particular areas of the world. (For more information about world markets, see Chapter 5.)

6A | MARKET RESEARCH:
COMPANIES, DATA, SURVEYS, AND REPORTS

San Francisco–based Community Marketing & Insights (CMI) is the leading LGBT marketing research company in North America. CMI's founder, Tom Roth, Senior Research Director David Paisley, and their team have quantified and tracked the LGBT market for over twenty years with the company's Annual Tourism and Hospitality Survey. The data gathered by this survey constitute a trusted resource, representing the best publicly available data on the LGBT population. Along with other respected research and marketing firms, including Out Now Global, CMI measures and tracks a huge amount of data in an increasingly wide range of industries. For example, CMI's proprietary survey panel, first developed in 1994, gathers data from 170 partner organizations around the world.

In addition, CMI has built a panel of 70,000 self-identifying LGBT community members, including 50,000 LGBT panelists in the United States, 6,500 LGBT Canadians, and 4,500 LGBT Chinese. In the United States, CMI's research can be divided into subcategories that include bisexuals, lesbians, millennials, and other groups. CMI offers custom research projects for clients who want to evaluate the market's potential, to identify market perceptions, or measure awareness before launching a campaign. CMI then helps these companies measure the effectiveness of their marketing over time.

"Twenty years ago, the travel and alcohol industries were the first industry segments to start reaching out to the LGBT community," says David Paisley. "Today, almost all consumer industries have some representation within LGBT outreach. It was the travel market that started LGBT marketing, and if we look at where the travel industry has gone over the last two decades with LGBT marketing, it could be an indication of where some other industry segments may get to at some point; but those industries are not there yet."

Most LGBT conventions tend to offer useful introductory sessions to help businesses gain familiarity with the market. For more advanced marketers, other organizations and resources provide a platform for deepening engagement with LGBT travel consumers around the globe. Where it is appropriate, we indicate in what ways each organization is ideal for marketers.

ABRAT-GLS (ABRATGLS.COM.BR)

This is the leading association in Brazil that connects the Brazilian tourism, leisure, and entertainment markets. A comprehensive website connects members to marketing opportunities, travel suppliers, and media.

GAY EUROPEAN TOURISM ASSOCIATION (GETA-EUROPE.ORG)

Created for businesses interested in the European market, this group offers members the resources to acquire more customers with marketing and networking and to improve business products and services with research, advice, and information.

Ideal for:

- Marketing
- Media directory
- Advice

INTERNATIONAL GAY AND LESBIAN TRAVEL ASSOCIATION (IGLTA.ORG)

Based in the United States, the International Gay and Lesbian Travel Association is a global travel network dedicated to connecting and educating LGBT travelers and the businesses that welcome and support them.

Ideal for:

- Exposure to the LGBT travel industry
- Annual global convention and website marketing

MEXICO'S LGBT COMMERCE AND TOURISM CONFEDERATION (MGLCC) (MGLCC.MX)

The MGLCC focuses on the promotion of Mexico's destinations to the national and international LGBT community, as well as Mexico's companies and services that target this segment exclusively or are considered gay-friendly. MGLCC's goals are to join forces with businesses and associations and to create mutual-cooperation agreements in order to form strong alliances and boost the LGBT segment in everything related to commerce and tourism.

NATIONAL LESBIAN AND GAY JOURNALISTS ASSOCIATION (NLGJA.ORG)

The U.S.-based NLGJA is an organization of journalists, media professionals, educators, and students working within the news industry to foster fair and accurate coverage of LGBT issues. NLGJA opposes all forms of workplace bias and provides professional development to its members. It sponsors an annual conference with programming and networking opportunities that may be of interest to marketers, especially those responsible for communications and media relations. The LGBT Media Summit leading into the annual NLGJA conference is a gathering of the top LGBT publishers and journalists in the United States. The organization's website includes a style book that provides guidance when writing about LGBT issues as well as an index of key terms.

Ideal for:

- Identifying and building relationships with key LGBT journalists
- LGBT Media Summit at the annual conference

6C | ADVOCACY ORGANIZATIONS

The following domestic and international organizations work for LGBT rights in society and the workplace.

ALTURI (ALTURI.ORG)

In the United States we have seen lesbian, gay, bisexual, transgender, and intersex rights and well-being advance over the past several decades. But LGBTI people are still criminalized, victimized, and discriminated against in every corner of the globe.

RIKA JEAN-FRANÇOIS, COMMISSIONER, ITB CORPORATE SOCIAL RESPONSIBILITY AND COMPETENCE CENTRE TRAVEL & LOGISTICS, ITB BERLIN, MESSE BERLIN, GERMANY

Q Can you talk about how the LGBT presence has grown at ITB Berlin, what the strategy has been, and what role you've played?

A ITB Berlin started in 1997 with a party and scattered LGBT exhibitors. Key West was first to have the rainbow flag. By 2005 there was our first joint booth. We worked with the community and got to know the key players. By 2010 we were ready to establish LGBT as a segment equal to other segments, similar to youth travel or adventure travel, and take it out of its niche. Now ITB Berlin features the LGBT Pavilion, called unofficially the Pink Pavilion (see Figure 22).

Q What was the time line and budget set against the LGBT initiative?

A It is part of the general budget, but it is not a big budget. What you need is a lot of personal dedication. In addition to budget, you need someone personally engaged and to have an international presence. When I'm engaged it's not because I'm personally involved, it is because corporate responsibility is part of responsible tourism. LGBT has been institutionalized at ITB.

Q What would you say are the top reasons the gay presence has succeeded in the conference?

A 1. Market demand and the spending capacity of LGBT travelers.
2. Professionalism of the LGBT enterprises. I think a lot of people working in the LGBT space are very professional. They are serious business people.
3. Dedication and authenticity of the people and the experience.
4. Marketing and PR have improved.

Q Was there any controversy or backlash about having a gay presence at ITB?

A Oh, yes, there was. In the beginning, some fellow exhibitors didn't want to be in the same "neighborhood" as the LGBT exhibitors. What changed that apprehension was education and clarification of facts. People fear what they don't know. We had to reassure exhibitors that LGBT tourism is not about making people "gay" or sex tourism. In that first Pink Pavilion, everyone drank coffee together and saw there was a lot of traffic. And they didn't convert to gay!

6 C

Alturi was created to bring together a community to help improve the living conditions of LGBTI people globally by educating the public, engaging partners and allies, and encouraging and facilitating support.

Ideal for:

- Creating a megaphone for oppressed LGBT people around the world
- Connecting consumers in the United States with LGBT advocates around the world

OUT & EQUAL WORKPLACE ADVOCATES (OUTANDEQUAL.ORG)

Out & Equal Workplace Advocates, based in the United States, is the world's premier organization dedicated to achieving lesbian, gay, bisexual, and transgender workplace equality. Out & Equal collaborates with Fortune 1000 companies and government agencies to provide a safe, welcoming, and supportive environment for LGBT employees. At the annual Workplace Summit, employees and experts from around the world gather to share strategies and best practices for creating an equal workplace that is inclusive of all sexual orientations, gender identities, and expressions.

Ideal for:

- Interacting with Fortune 1000 decision makers (at the annual Workplace Summit)
- Best business practices beyond the tourism and hospitality industry

OUTRIGHT ACTION INTERNATIONAL (OUTRIGHTINTERNATIONAL.ORG)

OutRight, formerly known as the International Gay and Lesbian Human Rights Commission, partners directly with thousands of activists throughout the Global South (Africa, Latin America, and developing Asia, including the Middle East) to develop effective advocacy for LGBTQI rights. It offers training programs for partners and activists on tactics and strategies for LGBTQI rights documentation and advocacy. OutRight monitors and documents the discriminatory and life-threatening conditions that LGBTQI people face in order to spur action to stop human rights violations when they occur. It advocates globally, regionally, and nationally—from the United Nations to activists working on the ground.

Ideal for:

- Understanding the human and civil rights of LGBT people
- Helping the community in locations where they are suppressed or worse
- Opportunities to donate travel products for auction

UTOPIA (UTOPIA-ASIA.COM)

Utopia's mission is to improve the lives of Asian lesbians and gay men in order to build community and to foster a deeper understanding of gay life in Asia. The Utopia Asia website is the most comprehensive English-language resource for the many multifaceted LGBT subcultures of Asia.

Ideal for:

- Learning more about Asian LGBT communities

6D | CONFERENCES AND EXPOSITIONS

The following conferences and expositions are useful for learning more about LGBT peoples and markets.

FITUR LGBT (FITURGAYLGBT.COM/EN/)

FITUR (Spain's international tourism fair) has the second-largest LGBT section, just after ITB Berlin. Overall, FITUR is highly focused on Spain and Latin America, and the LGBT section is more focused on Spain and less so on international destinations than the LGBT sections at ITB Berlin and World Travel Market, but it is still good for the LGBT segment within that geography. Exhibiting at FITUR LGBT is pretty inexpensive.

Ideal for:

- Those interested in the Spanish LGBT market

GNETWORK360 (GNETWORK360.COM)

Held annually in South America, GNETWORK360 is a three-day business-to-business event. More than nine hundred attendees join together to share information and presentations, attend workshops and panel discussions, and learn about business opportunities within the LGBT niche market.

Ideal for:

- Businesses interested in South American and Latin American LGBT travel
- Focus on emerging international market segments

INTERNATIONAL CONFERENCE ON GAY AND LESBIAN TOURISM PRESENTED BY COMMUNITY MARKETING, INC. (LGBTTOURISMCONFERENCE.COM)

Community Marketing hosts an annual conference for tourism professionals to learn about the gay and lesbian market from the experts and the people behind the success stories. It's a platform for educating and networking among marketing and sales executives of tourism boards, convention and visitors bureaus, destination marketing organizations, accommodations, tour operators, events, agencies, and meeting planners.

Ideal for:

- Education at all levels
- Latest research findings
- Networking

IGLTA ANNUAL GLOBAL CONVENTION (IGLTA.ORG)

Rotating around the world, IGLTA's annual convention is an educational and networking event for LGBT tourism professionals connecting gay, lesbian, and gay-friendly travel and tourism suppliers and buyers. It offers numerous educational workshops and networking receptions.

Ideal for:

- Educational programs
- Buyer and supplier programs

ITB'S GAY & LESBIAN TRAVEL PAVILION (ITB-BERLIN.DE)

Held annually in Berlin, ITB's Gay & Lesbian Travel Pavilion presents the world's largest range of LGBT tourism products at any trade fair.

Ideal for:

- Meeting travel suppliers and buyers catering primarily to European travelers
- Educational sessions
- Sales

LGBT CONFEX, INTERNATIONAL BUSINESS FORUM (LGBTCONFEX.COM)

The LGBT Confex International Business Forum is Latin America's leading LGBT travel business conference and consumer expo event.

Ideal for:

• Businesses interested in the Mexican and other Latin American travel segments

THE ORIGINAL LGBT EXPO (THELGBTEXPO.COM)

Held in New York city, the Original LGBT Expo is the largest and longest-running LGBT consumer expo in the world. The event showcases LGBT business, entertainment, politics, arts, education, lifestyle, and travel; over three hundred exhibiting companies cater to all facets of the LGBT community. The Expo also includes hours of educational seminars and an entertainment stage and includes the Travel Pavilion, Wedding Pavilion, Family Pavilion, Small Business Pavilion, and Nonprofit Pavilion.

Ideal for:

• Mass consumer exposure in the New York State area
• Sales of travel products directly to consumers

TRAVEL GAY CANADA ANNUAL LGBT TOURISM CONFERENCE (TGCCONFERENCE.COM)

Held annually in different cities in Canada, Travel Gay Canada focuses on Canada, with a minor focus on the United States and other international destinations. Most who attend are middle to senior managers in the hospitality, travel, and tourism industries interested in expanding their LGBT market share and ensuring that they are ready to welcome LGBT guests. The greatest participation is from those involved in marketing, guest services, and human resources. Industry segments include accommodations, transportation, attractions, destinations (cities, regions, and provinces or states), and tourism schools (educators and students).

Ideal for:

• Marketers interested in the Canadian travel segment

Held annually in London, the World Travel Market attracts five thousand exhibitors from 186 countries and regions. Industry deals worth $2.5 billion (in a typical year) are sealed at the world's leading tourism event. At the official "Out Now Business Class Official LGBT Village," an exhibitor space at World Travel Market, visitors will find industry leaders in LGBT tourism development from LGBT Village exhibiting partners, including LGBT media and LGBT travel bloggers. Similar LGBT Villages take place at World Travel Market Latin America and World Travel Market Africa.

Ideal for:

- Buyers and suppliers of travel products
- Education, networking, and exposure
- Media

6E | FURTHER READING

For those interested in diving deeper into various aspects of LGBT tourism, consider these books.

Business Inside Out: Capturing Millions of Brand-Loyal Gay Consumers, by Robert Witeck and Wesley Combs (Chicago: Kaplan, 2006), is the authoritative book on a research-based approach; it provides real-life insights into the needs, attitudes, behaviors, and purchasing power of the LGBT community.

Gay and Lesbian Tourism: The Essential Guide for Marketing, by Jeff Guaracino (Boston: Elsevier, 2007), is the first-ever guide to marketing for LGBT tourism companies and professionals.

Gay Press, Gay Power: The Growth of LGBT Community Newspapers in America, by Tracy Baim et al. (Chicago: CreateSpace, 2012), investigates the synergies between the U.S. gay rights movement and the print publications that cover the LGBT community.

Gay Tourism: Culture, Identity and Sex, by Stephen Clift, Michael Luongo, and Carry Callister (Boston: Cengage, 2002), examines the range of cultural, social, psychological, and health issues facing gay men and lesbians on their travels.

Gay Travels in the Muslim World, by Michael Luongo (New York: Routledge, 2007), journeys where other gay travel books fear to tread—Muslim countries. This thought-provoking book tells both Muslim and non-Muslim gay men's stories of traveling in the Middle East during these difficult political times.

Three autobiographies, while not specifically focused on travel, provide insight into media, military, and sports. A fourth book looks more closely at the world of gay sporting competition.

And Then I Danced: Traveling the Road to LGBT Equality, by Mark Segal (Brooklyn, N.Y.: OpenLens, 2015), is the life story of Mark Segal, the dean of American gay journalism over the last five decades. From the Stonewall demonstrations in 1969 to the founding of the *Philadelphia Gay News,* his life story is a must-read, first-person account of LGBT history.

Inside Out: Straight Talk from a Gay Jock (Mississauga, Ont.: Wiley, 2006) is the life story of the gold-medal-winning Olympic swimmer Mark Tewksbury. His book tells his personal story but also dives into the world of LGBT sports, including the controversial fight between the World Out Games and the Federation of Gay Games. Both the World Out Games and the Gay Games are sporting competitions that are tourism drivers and image builders; they are very important to destinations seeking to put themselves on the LGBT travel map.

Our Time: Breaking the Silence of Don't Ask, Don't Tell, edited by Josh Seefried (New York: Penguin, 2011), is a collection of stories of U.S. military service members confronting the now-rescinded "Don't Ask, Don't Tell" policy. Seefried is the cofounder of the military association Out Serve, which holds an annual conference in the United States.

The Outsports Revolution: Truth & Myth in the World of Gay Sports, by Jim Buzinski and Cyd Zeigler Jr. (Los Angeles: Alyson Books, 2007), is a compendium of the issues facing gay men and lesbians in the world of professional sports.

6F | ANNOTATED BIBLIOGRAPHY

By Oskaras Vorobjovas-Pinta, Tasmanian School of Business and Economics, University of Tasmania, Australia

Oskaras Vorobjovas-Pinta is a Ph.D. candidate at the University of Tasmania, Australia. His research interests are the sociology of tourism, neo-tribal behavior, and gay tourism. His research focuses on gay travelers as neo-tribes who come together from disparate walks of life but are united through shared sentiment, rituals, and symbols. In his research he has applied critical ethnography to explore the sociality and space of gay travelers in gay resorts in Queensland, Australia.

INTRODUCTION

It is easy to imagine the gay tourist as a contemporary invention, but gay tourism is not a new phenomenon. Victorian-era records of early gay travel activities center on well-educated, upper-class homosexual men from northern Europe taking Grand Tours to the Mediterranean in search of exotic cultures, warmer climates, and the companionship of younger men. In the late nineteenth and early twentieth centuries, a specific gay tourism infrastructure, including cafés, cabarets, and salons, developed in Berlin, Paris, and London—early antecedents to Copenhagen, Sydney, and New York, which actively court the pink dollar today. Weimar Berlin was considered the "gay Mecca" and "Eldorado" during its time, as gay culture there flourished. It offered a safe haven for both locals and travelers, who ventured there to escape the hetero-sexual world and express their sexuality.

The last four decades have seen a tremendous increase in academic research into LGBT travel. In the late 1980s, 1990s, and early 2000s, gay tourists started to be characterized as early adopters, trendsetters, innovators, and connoisseurs. During those decades, the gay consumer market was sometimes labeled a "dream market" and an "untapped gold mine." Despite these upbeat descriptions, however, other early research into gay tourists and their lives emerged from the HIV/AIDS crisis, pointing out the stigmatizing connotations of the disease and the moral panic of the times.

The early research tended to focus on the motivations and demographic profiles of gay tourists, as well as destination choices and the use of gay space. It was suggested that LGBT destinations such as Sitges in Spain or Key West in Florida give gay travelers the opportunity to escape the imposed heteronormativity of their everyday lives and to temporarily "come out" safely and anonymously. In recent years the increased visibility and acceptance of LGBT people, as well as the emergence of new technology, have prompted researchers to revisit the motivations and the profile of the "gay tourist" and to better appreciate the wide diversity of the people captured under the umbrella term *LGBT traveler*.

The last decade has been marked by the unprecedented pace of legal change for LGBT people in Western societies. From *Lawrence v. Texas* in 2003 to the groundbreaking legalization of same-sex marriage across the United States in 2015, that twelve-year window has seen a transition from decriminalization in some regions to wholesale legal assimilation. The relevance of the new laws to gay tourism operations cannot be overstated, as the tide of social and legal acceptance has permitted the business of gay travel to be conducted openly and with pride in more regions than ever before.

All this said, the great "coming out" of Western countries has been matched by—and may have indeed prompted—regression in the social and legal status of LGBT people in other parts of the world. As such, and as ever, understanding the needs of LGBT people is a complex undertaking. LGBT travelers must negotiate the cultural, legal, and societal norms of their travel destinations, and in this sense the rapid pace of change also represents uncertainty for the gay travel market and requires more and better research by academics in the field.

Most of the early literature focused on gay male travelers. Now there is a growing body of literature that incorporates the voices of lesbians, trans people, older gay travelers, and rainbow families.

EVENT TOURISM

Johnston, Lynda. *Queering Tourism: Paradoxical Performances at Gay Pride Parades.* **New York: Routledge, 2005.**

This book explores Gay Pride parades as tourist events through the intersection of sexuality, space, and tourism. The author explores the paradoxical relationships between the viewer and the viewed, as well as notions of bodily difference and the emerging new perceptions of power and tourism. The author based the book on a comprehensive collection of interviews, media accounts, photographs, advertisements, and her own involvement in the Pride parades in Australia, Italy, New Zealand, and Scotland.

Waitt, Gordon R. "Boundaries of Desire: Becoming Sexual through the Spaces of Sydney's 2002 Gay Games." *Annals of the Association of American Geographers* **96, no. 4 (2006): 773–787.**

The author explores experiences of male desire within the nonheterosexualized space in the context of the Sydney 2002 Gay Games. The paper revisits the spatial metaphor of "GLQBTI borderland" and reconsiders the relationship among desire, boundaries, imagined space, and sexualities. The article concludes by suggesting that sexual identities are actively and spatially constructed through processes that concurrently rationalize and resist social borders.

HOSPITALITY (HOTEL/MOTEL/LODGINGS)

Berezan, Orie, Carola Raab, Anjala S. Krishen, and Curtis Love. "Loyalty Runs Deeper Than Thread Count: An Exploratory Study of Gay Guest Preferences and Hotelier Perceptions." *Journal of Travel & Tourism Marketing* **32, no. 8 (2015): 1034–1050.**

In this article the authors explore some factors that define a truly gay-friendly hotel. They question whether hotels know how to effectively target the gay market. The study presents the ways a variety of hotel attributes requested by gay clientele influence the hotel-selection process.

Johnson, Corey W., and Diane M. Samdahl. " 'The Night They Took Over': Misogyny in a Country-Western Gay Bar." *Leisure Sciences* 27, no. 4 (2005): 331–348.

This article examines how gay men negotiate hegemonic masculinity in the context of a Lesbian Night at an American country-western gay bar. The authors reveal that the attitudes toward Lesbian Night, when women outnumber men, are based on the misogynistic assumptions deeply embedded within gay men's minds. The article concludes that leisure spaces are complex and dynamic locations that promote not only community but also a degree of inequality.

Ro, Heejung, Youngsoo Choi, and Eric D. Olson. "Service Recovery Evaluations: GLBT versus Hetero Customers." *International Journal of Hospitality Management* 33 (2013): 366–375.

This article analyzes and compares LGBT and heterosexual customers' perceptions of service encounters. Particularly, the authors explore customers' evaluation of service recovery in a hotel setting and examine whether the perceptions of LGBT and heterosexual customers differ. The findings suggest that LGBT customers' recovery evaluation is more positively inclined than that of their heterosexual counterparts. The authors consider the potential implications for hospitality managers on the basis of these findings.

LEISURE

Browne, Kath, and Leela Bakshi. "We Are Here to Party? Lesbian, Gay, Bisexual, and Trans Leisurescapes beyond Commercial Gay Scenes." *Leisure Studies* 30, no. 2 (2011): 179–196.

Browne and Bakshi attempt to comprehend the role of social networks and their influence on the process of normalization of leisure spaces. They argue that in light of an increased acceptance of homosexual lives, LGBT leisure spaces can no longer be limited or debated only in terms of a heterosexual-homosexual dichotomy. The authors assert that spaces can be concurrently gay and straight, yet they acknowledge that sexual and gender identities remain crucial even when such identities are "accepted" in predominantly heterosexual leisure spaces.

Giovanardi, Massimo, Andrea Lucarelli, and Patrick L'Espoir Decosta. "Co-performing Tourism Places: The 'Pink Night' Festival." *Annals of Tourism Research* 44 (2014): 102–115.

Adopting an ecological perspective, this article explores the practices and processes that stem from the relationship between residents and tourists. The authors analyze the encounter between "hosts" and "guests" by examining the case of the Pink Night, an annual festival held along the Emilia-Romagna coastal region in Italy. Their findings suggest that the festival space is a point of convergence among locals, tourists, and tourism workers, who cooperate to make Pink Night a success.

Hindle, Paul. "Gay Communities and Gay Space in the City." In *The Margins of the City: Gay Men's Urban Lives,* edited by Stephen Whittle, 7–25. Aldershot, U.K.: Arena Press, 1994.

This book chapter examines the components of a gay community and the role of gay space. The author uses Manchester's Gay Village as a case study and compares it with San Francisco's gay culture. Hindle sees gay space as the "physical manifestation of gay community." Essentially, he argues that gay leisure venues such as gay bars, as well as entire gay districts, provide a sense of safety and freedom from the constraints of a wider society. Hindle also poses the question of whether the development of gay districts will result in further segregation and the establishment of a ghettolike situation, or whether such districts will be integrated into the whole community.

Visser, Gustav. "Challenging the Gay Ghetto in South Africa: Time to Move On?" *Geoforum* 49 (2013): 268–274.

Visser argues that in light of social and institutional acceptance of homosexuals, the role and the perception of gay leisure spaces started changing. Arguably, these changes have resulted in the "de-gaying" of gay leisure spaces and the emergence of new forms of leisure spaces, such as mixed, gay-friendly, and post-gay. The author concludes that Western theorization of the links between gay sexual identity and space is not universally applicable.

Visser, Gustav. "Gay Men, Leisure Space, and South African Cities: The Case of Cape Town." *Geoforum* 34, no. 1 (2003): 123–137.

In this article Visser analyzes the meaning and effect of gay leisure space development in De Waterkant, a suburb of Cape Town, South Africa. The author argues that this renowned "gay village" is like an enclave and does not welcome the majority of gay South Africans. He further claims that gay spaces in De Waterkant are primarily designed for wealthier white male gays, which is a consequence of the legacy of apartheid.

Visser, Gustav. "The Homonormalization of White Heterosexual Leisure Spaces in Bloemfontein, South Africa." *Geoforum* 39, no. 3 (2008): 1347–1361.

This article reviews and analyzes the development of gay male leisure space in South Africa. The author pays attention to the relationship between sexual identity and leisure space, concluding that in light of an increased institutional and sociocultural acceptance of gay people, the image of gay leisure spaces (such as the ones in Bloemfontein) can start to show signs of homonormalizing as well.

Visser, Gustav. "Urban Tourism and the De-gaying of Cape Town's De Waterkant." *Urban Forum* 25, no. 4 (2014): 469–482.

This article examines the relationship between urban tourism and sexuality and how it affects historically white neighborhoods. Furthermore, the author explores the intersection between sexual identity and leisure seeking and its effect on the changing geographies of the De Waterkant neighborhood in South Africa. The paper questions the sociocultural and historical integrity of the neighborhood and concludes that De Waterkant has gone through striking changes that exclude a broad spectrum of urban dwellers.

Weeden, Clare, Jo-Anne Lester, and Nigel Jarvis. "Lesbians and Gay Men's Vacation Motivations, Perceptions, and Constraints: A Study of Cruise Vacation Choice." *Journal of Homosexuality* (2016): 1–18.

This article looks at the travel motivations of gay and lesbian tourists and explores how these motivations influence purchasing behavior when choosing a mainstream or LGBT cruise. The study found that gay male tourists, unlike lesbians, tend to choose both mainstream and LGBT cruises. The article acknowledges that the LGBT cruise market is diverse and should not be confined to gay and lesbian travelers. Future research should explore the needs and wants of bisexual, transgender, and queer consumers.

TOURISM AND TRAVEL

Clift, Stephen, and Simon Forrest. "Gay Men and Tourism: Destinations and Holiday Motivations." *Tourism Management* 20, no. 5 (1999): 615–625.

This quantitative study offers findings on the tourist destinations and holiday motivations of 562 homosexual men based in southern England. The aspects of gay tourist motivation uncovered were "gay social life and sex," "culture and sights," and "comfort and relaxation."

Clift, Stephen, and John Wilkins. "Travel, Sexual Behavior, and Gay Men." In *AIDS: Safety, Sexuality, and Risk,* **edited by Peter Aggleton, Peter Davies, and Graham Hart, 35–54. London: Taylor & Francis, 1995.**

This book chapter presents a critical review of literature pertaining to sexual behavior and potential sexual health risks of gay men in the context of tourism. The authors question the integrity and methodological frameworks of previous studies and propose recommendations for future studies in the field.

Coon, David R. "Sun, Sand, and Citizenship: The Marketing of Gay Tourism." *Journal of Homosexuality* 59, no. 4 (2012): 511–534.

The paper discusses trends in gay and lesbian tourism. It suggests that while the proliferation of travel arrangements aimed at the LGBT community might indicate higher levels of social acceptance, some of the strategies employed by marketers still treat homosexual travelers as second-class citizens within a broader American society.

Hughes, Howard L. "A Gay Tourism Market." *Journal of Quality Assurance in Hospitality & Tourism* **5, nos. 2–4 (2005): 57–74.**

This article considers marketing approaches toward which gay travelers are argued to be responsive. Hughes claims that appropriate targeting of the gay travel market does have an effect on validating gay lifestyles. He further aims to unpack some of the more negative aspects associated with the escalation of the myth of the affluent and carefree gay consumer. These encompass such issues as a false sense of liberation and distraction from the quest for more fundamental aspects of equality.

Hughes, Howard L. "Holidays and Homosexual Identity." *Tourism Management* **18, no. 1 (1997): 3–7.**

This article makes the case that gay travel contributes to the construction of one's identity. Hughes suggests that for some, going on vacations is the only opportunity to temporarily "come out," be "authentic," and meet like-minded others. On the other hand, the situation where one can be authentic only in leisure rather than in a day-to-day context may result in the underdevelopment of one's identity.

Hughes, Howard L. "Lesbians as Tourists: Poor Relations of a Poor Relation." *Tourism and Hospitality Research* **7, no. 1 (2006): 17–26.**

The author suggests that most literature pertaining to gay tourism has focused on the motivations and travel behavior of gay men, and that there is a corresponding lack of research into the travel motivations of lesbian tourists. Hughes posits that the decision-making process of lesbian travelers is influenced primarily by considerations of gender, as opposed to sexual orientation. As such, the lesbian tourist profile is distinct from that of gay men and heterosexual women.

Hughes, Howard L. *Pink Tourism: Holidays of Gay Men and Lesbians.* **Oxfordshire: CABI, 2006.**

This book is Hughes's response to the lack of quality research within the field of gay tourism. It reviews the marketing aspect of gay and lesbian tourism. Hughes explores not only the effect of this marketing but also the levels of engagement and relational qualities between marketing activities and social aspects of everyday gay lives.

Hughes, Howard L., and Richard Deutsch. "Holidays of Older Gay Men: Age or Sexual Orientation as Decisive Factors?" *Tourism Management* **31, no. 4 (2010): 454–463.**

This article explores the sub-niche of older gay travelers and the existing diversity within the gay travel market. The study is based on interviews conducted with twenty-three men over the age of thirty-five. The results show that vacation requirements of older gay men are comparable to those of other older people; yet gay men are also seeking the element of gay friendliness. The authors feel that there are opportunities present for travel specialists and operators to develop products and for destinations to be positioned appropriately for the older gay men's market.

Monterrubio, J. Carlos. "Identity and Sex: Concurrent Aspects of Gay Tourism." *Tourismos: An International Multidisciplinary Journal of Tourism* 4, no. 2 (2009): 155–167.

Monterrubio critically reviews the existing gay travel literature and aims to establish the relationship between identity and sex in terms of gay tourism. This paper provides evidence that sex is a relevant and frequent facet in gay travel. The author concludes that tourism and the gay sexual identity are indeed inextricably linked.

Pritchard, Annette, Nigel J. Morgan, Diane Sedgely, and Andrew Jenkins. "Reaching Out to the Gay Tourist: Opportunities and Threats in an Emerging Market Segment." *Tourism Management* 19, no. 3 (1998): 273–282.

This article reviews the rise of the gay consumer profile and explores the emergence of gay-friendly travel products and destinations. It suggests that although the public space is contested, controlled, and by default predominantly heteronormative, there are great opportunities for reaching out to the gay consumer. The authors acknowledge, however, that increased tourist activity in gay spaces may result in the "de-gaying" process and, hence, hinder the concept of gay identity.

Pritchard, Annette, Nigel J. Morgan, Diane Sedgley, Elizabeth Khan, and Andrew Jenkins. "Sexuality and Holiday Choices: Conversations with Gay and Lesbian Tourists." *Leisure Studies* 19, no. 4 (2000): 267–282.

This article analyzes the travel motivations of gay and lesbian travelers on the basis of in-depth interviews and focus groups. It explores the interdependence of sexuality, tourism behavior, and tourism spaces. The authors argue that sexual orientation has a critical influence on the travel choices of gay and lesbian consumers. The findings suggest that gay and lesbian tourists travel with an intention to escape heterosexualized environments, to spend time with like-minded others, and to express their sexuality in a safe, nonjudgmental space.

Therkelsen, Anette, Bodil Stilling Blichfeldt, Jane Chor, and Nina Ballegaard. " 'I Am Very Straight in My Gay Life': Approaching an Understanding of Lesbian Tourists' Identity Construction." *Journal of Vacation Marketing* 19, no. 4 (2013): 317–327.

The authors argue that literature pertaining to gay travel research has focused mainly on gay male tourists. Hence, the paper explores lesbian tourists and how they diverge from a more traditional understanding of gay tourists. An important practical implication of the research is that the gay travel market is very diverse, and it needs to be approached in a nuanced and sensitive manner.

Vorobjovas-Pinta, Oskaras, and Anne Hardy, "The Evolution of Gay Travel Research." *International Journal of Tourism Research* 18, no. 4 (2016): 409–416.

This paper explores literature relating to the gay travel market. The authors argue that there is a lack of research on the outcomes of societal and technological change and increased acceptance of gay relationships and their effects on gay tourist motivations. It has been suggested that stereotyped and generalized projections of the motivations and social behaviors of gay travelers have perpetrated a distorted understanding of the gay travel market. With this in mind, the authors emphasize a number of significant opportunities for future research into the gay travel market.

Waitt, Gordon, and Kevin Markwell. *Gay Tourism: Culture and Context.* Binghamton, N.Y.: Haworth Hospitality Press, 2006.

This book explores the evolution of the commercial gay tourism industry. It details the organizational, managerial, political, and sociocultural aspects of the industry and examines the relation among gay tourism, Western gay male culture, the erotic, sexual politics, and sexual diversity.

DESTINATION CHOICES

Blichfeldt, Bodil Stilling, Jane Chor, and Nina Ballegaard Milan. " 'It Really Depends on Whether You Are in a Relationship': A Study of 'Gay Destinations' from a Tourist Perspective." *Tourism Today* 11 (Fall 2011): 7–26.

This article examines the appeal, meaning, and perceptions of gay tourist destinations. The authors argue that the choice of a gay destination might be influenced by such aspects as gay travelers' everyday life context, motivations, civil status, and identity. The qualitative study uncovered that there is no such thing as a "gay tourist," but, rather, there are some homosexual people who might choose to become "gay tourists" for a short period.

Blichfeldt, Bodil Stilling, Jane Chor, and Nina Ballegaard Milan. "Zoos, Sanctuaries, and Turfs: Enactments and Uses of Gay Spaces during the Holidays." *International Journal of Tourism Research* 15, no. 5 (2013): 473–483.

The research focuses on the concept of "gay space" and explains that some gay travelers use such spaces as sanctuaries. The key finding of this study is that gay space per se does not play a focal role but is, rather, perceived as an added bonus to a vacation. Furthermore, the study found that lesbians do not tend to frequent gay spaces during their vacations because of the preestablished assumptions that such spaces are predominantly masculine.

Hughes, Howard L. "Gay Men's Holiday Destination Choice: A Case of Risk and Avoidance." *International Journal of Tourism Research* 4, no. 4 (2002): 299–312.

This paper applies risk and destination avoidance approaches to explore the potential influence of discrimination and social disapproval on the choice of vacation destinations. It has been proposed that the perceived hostility toward homosexuals caused either by laws or by different cultural norms has had an effect on the travel geography of gay travelers. Gay men and women are indeed less likely to visit such countries or regions.

Hughes, Howard L. "Marketing Gay Tourism in Manchester: New Market for Urban Tourism or Destruction of 'Gay Space'?" *Journal of Vacation Marketing* 9, no. 2 (2003): 152–163.

This paper analyzes Manchester's marketing campaign targeted at the homosexual men's market. Hughes examines the potential influence of such a campaign on the significance of the city's "gay space." The study found that the marketing campaign was successful; however, it rested solely on the issues pertaining to gay space. Consequently, the situation has led to a shift of "ownership" of the Gay Village, and, hence, the perceived security of the local gay community has weakened.

Hughes, Howard L., Juan Carlos Monterrubio, and Amanda Miller. " 'Gay' Tourists and Host Community Attitudes." *International Journal of Tourism Research* 12, no. 6 (2010): 774–786.

The authors argue that despite the elevated academic and commercial interest in gay travelers, there is a lack of research in understanding the views of host communities toward such tourists. The paper explores the residents' perceptions of homosexual tourists in Zipolite, a small coastal Mexican town. The study found that the attitudes were predominantly positive; however, the locals have expressed concerns about the overt sexual behavior of gay travelers.

Lucena, Rodrigo, Nigel Jarvis, and Clare Weeden. "A Review of Gay and Lesbian Parented Families' Travel Motivations and Destination Choices: Gaps in Research and Future Directions." *Annals of Leisure Research* 18, no. 2 (2015): 1–18.

The authors point to the lack of research on gay-parented family tourism and explain that the majority of the existing gay travel literature has been centered on individual choices and decisions. The article presents an extensive literature review pertaining to same-sex-parented family tourism and uncovers the following four areas that require further research: travel motivations, destination choice, family decision making, and strategies used by lesbians and gay men to manage sexuality in public spaces.

Melián-González, Arturo, Sergio Moreno-Gil, and Jorge E. Araña. "Gay Tourism in a Sun and Beach Destination." *Tourism Management* 32, no. 5 (2011): 1027–1037.

This article portrays a differentiating profile of European gay travelers at a sun-and-beach destination. Furthermore, it analyzes a destination's competitiveness in attracting a specific segment by checking the validity of the resource-based view. The authors also use the innovative approach of Bayesian model averaging to destination competitiveness. The study's findings reveal that gay tourists rank good climate, gay scene, nightlife, and a gay-friendly environment as some of the most important aspects when choosing a travel destination.

Mendoza, Cristóbal. "Beyond Sex Tourism: Gay Tourists and Male Sex Workers in Puerto Vallarta (Western Mexico)." *International Journal of Tourism Research* 15, no. 2 (2013): 122–137.

This article examines the relationship between gay tourists and male sex workers in the coastal resort town of Puerto Vallarta, Mexico. The main purpose of this study was to explore the reasons and motivations of male sex workers for engaging in sex services aimed at a male clientele. The results show that male prostitution is based on an offer-and-demand principle and provides greater income opportunities than any other paid activities in the town. Furthermore, it has been posited that engagement in male sex services helps sex workers maintain their particular lifestyle. The author concludes that sexual practices are negotiated, but sexual identities are not.

Mitchell, Gregory. "TurboConsumers™ in Paradise: Tourism, Civil Rights, and Brazil's Gay Sex Industry." *American Ethnologist* 38, no. 4 (2011): 666–682.

The author analyzes the habits and routines of North American gay sex tourists in Brazil. Mitchell locates a tension between the appeal to these tourists of the exoticized difference of Brazilian understandings of same-sex desire and their politically motivated imposition of their own universalizing model of gay identity. These tourists pursue difference while simultaneously acting to diminish these same differences.

Monterrubio, Carlos, and Mercy Barrios-Ayala. "Holiday Motivations: Conversations with Lesbians in Mexico." *International Journal of Tourism Sciences* 15, nos. 1–2 (2015): 22–29.

This paper explains that most of the studies pertaining to homosexual travelers have been focused on gay men. The purpose of the study was to explore the travel motivations of Mexican lesbian travelers. The findings suggest that in addition to sexuality, a variety of other factors, such as cultural experiences and strengthening family ties, form the vacation experiences of lesbians.

DISCUSSION QUESTION

1. How can your organization effectively make use of some of the tips provided here to keep your LGBT marketing campaign competitive?

NOTES

NOTES TO CHAPTER 1

1 Flora Drury, "Horrific Moment Two Gay Men Are Thrown Off Tall Building by ISIS Then Stoned by Baying Mob Including Children," *Daily Mail,* August 14, 2015, www.dailymail.co.uk/news/article-3198283 /Horrific-moment-two-gay-men-thrown-tall-building-ISIS-stoned-baying-mob-including-children .html.

2 Katy Steinmetz, "Why Transgender People Are Being Murdered at a Historic Rate," *Time,* August 17, 2015, http://time.com/3999348/transgender-murders-2015.

3 U.N. General Assembly, Human Rights Council, "Discriminatory Laws and Practices and Acts of Violence against Individuals Based on Their Sexual Orientation and Gender Identity," November 17, 2011, 13, www.ohchr.org/Documents/Issues/Discrimination/A.HRC.19.41_English.pdf.

4 Kieran Guilbert, "Activists Fear Law Leaves Young LGBT Feeling Isolated," Reuters, September 14, 2015, http://news.trust.org/item/20150914000140-wx20w.

5 Mehmet Caliskan and Yesmin Dikmen, "Turkish Police Use Water Cannon to Disperse Gay Pride Parade," **Reuters,** June 28, 2015, http://uk.reuters.com/article/uk-turkey-rights-pride-idUKKCN0P80P420150628.

6 "Cosmopolitan Responds to Backlash over Report on Banned Transgender Guest," *Las Vegas Sun,* April 27, 2011, http://lasvegassun.com/news/2011/apr/27/cosmopolitan-responds-backlash-over-report -banned-/.

7 Ibid.

8 Randy Bennett, "Not for Bim: Barbados Not Pursuing Gay Tourists," *Barbados Today,* July 18, 2015, http:// www.barbadostoday.bb/2015/07/18/not-for-bim/.

9 James B. Stewart, "Exxon Lumbers Along to Catch Up with Gay Rights," *New York Times,* July 1, 2015, http://www.nytimes.com/2015/07/02/business/exxon-lumbers-along-to-catch-up-with-gay-rights .html?_r=0.

10 Out Now Global LGBT 2030 Report, "The Power of Friends: How LGBT Allies Are Transforming Business and Society."

11 LGBT Capital, press release, August 3, 2015, www.lgbt-capital.com/docs/LGBT-GDP_2015_Press_Release .pdf.

12 Gary J. Gates, "Gay People Count, So Why Not Count Them Correctly?" *Washington Post,* April 8, 2011, www .washingtonpost.com/opinions/gay-people-count-so-why-not-count-them-correctly/2011/04/07/AFD g9K4C_story.html.

13 Maria Tadeo, "Rich Gay Men Wanted: Spain's Conservatives Make Tourist Appeal," *Bloomberg Business,* August 31, 2015, www.bloomberg.com/news/articles/2015-08-31/rich-gay-men-wanted-spain-s-con servatives-make-tourist-appeal.

14 Garrett Sloane, "How Facebook Showed Live Nation That Grindr Ads Sell Madonna Tickets," *Adweek,* June 25, 2015, www.adweek.com/news/technology/how-facebook-showed-live-nation-grindr-ads-sell -madonna-tickets-165582.

NOTES TO CHAPTER 2

1 Merryn Johns presentation, LGBT Week, New York, April 2015.

2 Out Now's Global LGBT 2030 study, "The Power of Friends: How LGBT Allies Are Transforming Business and Society."

NOTES TO CHAPTER 3

1 Guaracino, *Gay and Lesbian Tourism,* 58–59.

2 "Aspen Gay Ski Week 2017," http://gayskiweek.com/.

3 Whistler Municipality, Economic Impact Assessment, May 2013.

4 European Gay and Lesbian Sports Federation, www.eglsf.info.

5 "World Outgames," Outgames.org.

6 See Federation of Gay Games, www.gaygames.org.

7 InterPride, www.interpride.org.

8 The Center for Black Equity, centerforblackequity.org.

9 Andrew Lear, Oscar Wilde Tours, www.oscarwildetours.com.

10 NYBG newsletter, October 2015, www.nybg.org/frida/evenings.html.

11 Michael Luongo, "Vatican Art in a Gay Light," *New York Times,* December 31, 2014, www.nytimes.com /2015/01/04/travel/vatican-art-in-a-gay-light.html.

12 Alessio Virgili, e-mail to the authors, April 18, 2016.

13 "Cruise Line Survey 2015," *ManAboutWorld,* http://www.manaboutworld.com/cruise-line-survey-2015/.

14 Ibid.

15 Ed Salvato, "Cultivating the LGBT Travel Business," American Bus Association, www.pohlyco.com /wp-content/uploads/2015/08/15-AB1-408.insider0817.1.pdf.

16 Aaron Cooper, "Alaska Airlines Ends Prayer Cards on Flights," *CNN Belief Blog,* January 26, 2012, http:// religion.blogs.cnn.com/2012/01/26/alaska-airlines-ends-prayer-cards-on-flights.

17 Clint Ostler, presentation at CMI's Sixteenth Conference on LGBT Tourism & Hospitality in Fort Lauderdale, Florida, December 2015.

18 This case study is based on the authors' interviews with Randy Griffin (at the time of publication of this book, executive vice president of sales and marketing for Marshall Hotels and Resorts) and Bob Witeck (president and founder of Witeck Communications, Inc., formerly Witeck-Combs Communications, Inc.).

19 "List of LGBT-Related Organizations and Conferences," https://en.wikipedia.org/wiki/List_of_LGBT -related_organizations_and_conferences.

20 Guaracino, *Gay and Lesbian Tourism,* 128.

21 "Out&Equal Workplace Summit," outandequal.org/events/summit/.

22 "Mission," galachoruses.org/about/mission.

23 "Creating Change," thetaskforce.org/creating-change/.

24 John Tanzella, e-mail to the authors, March 15, 2016.

25 Guaracino, *Gay and Lesbian Tourism,* 56.

26 "Meeting Industry United in Condemning Indiana Religious Freedom Law," *USAE News,* April 7, 2015.

27 Alan Blinder and Richard Pérea-Peña, "Kentucky Clerk Denies Same-Sex Marriage Licenses, Defying Court," *New York Times,* September 1, 2015; Joel Landau and Ginger Adams Otis, "Kentucky Clerk Kim Davis Released from Prison," *New York Daily News,* October 1, 2015, www.nydailynews.com/news/crime /kim-davis-freer-americans-lawyer-article-1.2352035; and Stephanie Kirchgaessner, "Vatican: Pope Did Not Show Support for Kim Davis," *Guardian,* October 2, 2015, www.theguardian.com/world/2015 /oct/02/vatican-pope-kim-davis-same-sex-marriage.

28 Associated Press, "Northern Indiana Pizzeria That Backed Religious Law Reopens," *South Florida Gay News,* April 10, 2015, https://southfloridagaynews.com/National/northern-indiana-pizzeria-that-backed-reli gious-law-reopens.html.

29 Henry McDonald, "Bert and Ernie Gay Marriage Cake Refused by Northern Ireland Bakery," *Guardian,* July 8, 2014, https://www.theguardian.com/uk-news/2014/jul/08/bert-and-ernie-gay-wedding-cake -northern-ireland-ashers-bakery.

30 Dan McCue, "The 'So Gay' Episode Sets South Carolina Back Decades," *Charleston City Paper,* 2008, www .charlestoncitypaper.com/charleston/the-so-gay-episode-sets-south-carolina-back-decades/Content ?oid=1116259; Huma Khan and Eric Noe, "Mark Sanford's Emails Detail His Argentine Affair," *ABC News,* June 24, 2009, http://abcnews.go.com/Politics/story?id=7916857&page=1; and Liz Lohuis, "Sena-tor: University Program Designed to Recruit Lesbians," *WYFF4.com,* April 7, 2014, www.wyff4.com/news /controversy-continues-over-gaythemed-material-at-upstate-university/25350080.

31 Frank Ahrens, "Disney's Theme Weddings Come True for Gay Couples," *Washington Post,* April 7, 2007.

32 Richard Hack, "Family OutFest: Disney Backs New LGBT-Inclusive Family Vacation," *Florida Agenda,* October 25, 2015.

NOTES TO CHAPTER 4

1 Robert Klara, "Gay Advertising's Long March Out of the Closet," *Ad Week,* June 16, 2013, www.adweek .com/news/advertising-branding/gay-advertising-s-long-march-out-closet-150235.

2 Ibid.

3 Stuart Elliott, "The Top 5 Changes on Madison Ave. over the Last 25 Years," *New York Times,* Decem-ber 18, 2014, www.nytimes.com/2014/12/19/business/media/the-top-5-changes-on-madison-ave-over -the-last-25-years.html?_r=0.

4 Klara, "Gay Advertising's Long March Out of the Closet."

5 Navigaytour, http://navigaytour.net.

6 Interview with Mark Segal, February 15, 2016.

7 "Everything's Sexier in Paris," rrpartners.com/work/everythings-sexier-in-paris.

8 Interview with Michael Bertetto, October 2015.

9 Stuart Elliott, "Commercials with a Gay Emphasis Are Moving to Mainstream Media," *New York Times,* June 25, 2013, www.nytimes.com/2013/06/26/business/media/commercials-with-a-gay-emphasis-are -moving-to-mainstream-media.html?_r=0.

10 Interview with Scott Gatz, November 2015.

11 Ibid.

12 Gay Ad Network, www.gayadnework.com.

13 Interview with Steve Levin, October 2015.

14 Jamie Tabberer, "Gay App SCRUFF to Launch New Travel Feature, Venture," *GayStarNews,* October 21, 2015, www.gaystarnews.com/article/gay-app-scruff-to-launch-new-travel-feature-venture.

NOTES TO CHAPTER 5

1 Guaracino, *Gay and Lesbian Tourism,* 149.

2 "The 'Queer of the Year'—Could It Be You?" Tourisme Montreal, June 24, 2010, http://www.tourisme -montreal.org/blog/the-queer-of-the-year-could-it-be-you/.

3 Noa Sapir, head of Incoming Tourism, Tel Aviv government.

4 Japan National Tourism Board, Annual Report, 2014.

5 Shiho Ikeuchi, "Promoting Japan as a LGBT-Friendly Destination," *Acumen,* July 2015, https://bccjacu men.com/promoting-japan-as-a-lgbt-friendly-destination.

6 Statistics provided by Visit Philadelphia to various news organizations, including Media Post; Karl Greenberg, "Philly Extends Social-Media Push to LGBT Travelers," Media Post, November 5, 2012, www .mediapost.com/publications/article/186572/philly-extends-social-media-push-to-lgbt-travelers.html.

INDEX

Page references followed by italicized *t*. indicate tables. Emboldened **fig.** or **figs.** indicates color plates or material contained in their captions.

NOTES

NOTES

NOTES

NOTES

NOTES

NOTES

NOTES

NOTES

NOTES

NOTES

NOTES

NOTES